Teradata Toolbox

Steve Savoye

Steve Wilmes

First Edition

Cerulium Corporation
www.cerulium.com

Copyright

ISBN: 978-0-9820871-5-2
Printed by PrintRS, Inc.

Trademarks

The following are registered names and/or trademarks, used throughout this book:

Teradata, Teradata BYNET, Teradata Administrator, and Teradata SQL Assistant are registered trademarks and/or products of Teradata Corporation.

Microsoft Windows, Windows Server, Windows XP, Windows Vista, Windows 7, and MS-DOS, .NET, SQL Server are either registered trademarks or trademarks of Microsoft Corporation.

DEC, VAX, and VMS are registered trademarks of Digital Equipment Corporation.

Intel, Pentium, Xeon are registered trademarks of the Intel Corporation.

Ethernet is a trademark of the Xerox Corporation.

AT&T is a registered trademark of the AT&T Corporation.

NCR is a registered trademark of the NCR Corporation.

IBM, CICS, DB2, MVS, RACF, OS/390, Tivoli, WebSphere, and VM are registered trademarks of International Business Machines Corporation.

UNIX is a registered trademark of The Open Group.

Linux is a registered trademark of Linus Torvalds.

Unicode is a registered trademark of Unicode, Inc.

Sun Microsystems, Sun Java, Solaris, SPARC, and Sun are trademarks or registered trademarks of Sun Microsystems, Inc. in the U.S. or other countries.

NetVault is a trademark and BakBone is a registered trademark of BakBone Software, Inc.

NetBackup and VERITAS are trademarks of VERITAS Software Corporation.

In addition to these product names, all brand and product names in this manual are trademarks of their respective holders in the United States and/or other countries.

Dedications

I dedicate this book to my wife, Becky, and to my family, who inspired me to write and publish this book. I also acknowledge all those – you know who you are – that assisted in making this book a reality. Thank you again.

--Steve Wilmes

This book is dedicated to my wife Jill and to my three children, who have truly sacrificed to make this happen. In addition, I give special thanks to my business colleagues, who supported this effort. Lastly, I give praise to my Lord and Savior for his guidance, support, love, and strength each day.

--Steve Savoye

About the Author – Steve Savoye

Steve Savoye currently serves as a Senior Database Administrator for a prominent healthcare company in North Carolina. Steve has almost 20 years of experience in the IT field and has worked with Teradata systems since an Oracle to Teradata migration in 2002.

His primary responsibilities include performance monitoring and tuning, database administration, capacity planning, and project integration for his company's Enterprise Data Warehouse. Prior to his current position, Steve assumed several roles in programming, management, and Database Administration at AT&T.

Mr. Savoye graduated from Rutgers in 1990 with a BA in computer Science and Economics, then from Fairleigh Dickinson University in 1995 with an MBA in Information Management. Steve joined the Teradata Service Focus Team in 2005 and is a Teradata Certified Master.

Mr. Savoye resides in Raleigh, North Carolina, with his wife Jill and their 3 children who are all under 4 years of age. Outside of work and home, Steve is actively involved in his church and with Habitat for Humanity. He enjoys playing golf, basketball and tennis, but finding time to do any of these is quite difficult these days.

About the Author – Steve Wilmes

Steve Wilmes founded Cerulium Corporation in 2007. As Chief Executive Officer, his goal is to establish Cerulium as a premier data warehousing technology company. Cerulium's strategic growth is globally focused on six lines of business including education, consulting, BI solutions, productivity tools, application integration and assessment services. These lines of business have been highly successful by utilizing strategic data warehousing solutions provided by Teradata that spans across the consumer, and commercial markets.

Mr. Wilmes has over 20 years of experience in the computer industry and is known to be a detail oriented, results-focused leader. He is an internationally recognized expert in several aspects of data warehousing including hardware, software, SQL, operating systems, implementation, data integration, database administration, and BI solutions.

Mr. Wilmes earned a bachelor's degree in business administration and economics in 1994 from Augsburg College and he is also a Teradata Certified Master.

Mr. Wilmes resides just outside of Columbia, South Carolina, with his wife, Becky. He has been involved with numerous civic, educational, and business organizations throughout his career. Some of his more recent associations include working with the Richland County Sheriff's Department – Region 4 Community Member, and volunteer for local organizations where he shares his technical expertise.

Contents

Introduction

This book is the culmination of decades of professional work in Teradata and Database Administration. With so many methods for accomplishing the same result, the experience reflected in this book will help the reader rapidly adopt an efficient approach to solving many Teradata related problems. Consider this book a compilation of lessons learned so others won't have to learn the hard way. Readers of this book will benefit from the experience and mistakes of those who have already been there, done that, and bought the T-shirt. Don't reinvent the wheel if it's not needed.

This book provides real solutions, approaches and insight to a variety of issues and topics. Reference manuals and websites have their place, but they don't always give adequate instruction or relevant examples. This book is intended to fill that gap and serve as a complement to reference material and guides.

Every Teradata customer needs to perform software upgrades. This book provides an extensive list of steps needed to perform upgrades, and these steps can be used as a checklist during upgrades. These are best practices that everyone should incorporate.

All Database management systems require the collection of statistics, and in Teradata, it is of the utmost importance. Suggestions are given on just how, when, why and on what to collect. We will illustrate one particular approach or solution that addresses the how, when, why, and what. Limitations are discussed as well.

This book also illustrates approaches to securing databases, tables and views. There are several ways to secure each, and we offer a few ways to get started. Included in the text are working macros and stored procedures to automate the creation of views.

Readers are provided guidelines to become proficient at programming procedures because there are a multitude of uses for them. We discuss some best practices and concerns when writing stored procedures.

No system can be without an infrastructure for maintaining users either. It is imperative to write stored procedures or processes to create users, maintain passwords, adjust spool allocations, assign privileges and roles, change security, etc. This book will help you establish divisions of responsibilities and offload some of the repetitive work that DBAs get inundated with to those performing operational activities.

Finally, this book was written after fielding thousands of questions over many years. It's intended to give best practices, possible alternatives and approaches, and ignite the brainstorming process to solve specific challenges. It is also aimed at making the reader aware of possible limitations and road blocks along the way. We hope this material is found to be beneficial no matter what your level of Teradata mastery. Please feel free to send us your comments, whether good or bad, and thanks for reading.

Chapter 1: Basics of Teradata Data Warehousing

What is a Teradata Database?

Scaleable
Linear
Business Intelligent
Data Warehousing

The Teradata® Database is a Relational Database Management System (RDBMS), manufactured by the Teradata Corporation, and is designed to support databases ranging from less than one terabyte to those with thousands of terabytes. This makes Teradata an obvious choice for both mid-range and very large data warehousing applications. With its parallelism and scalability, Teradata allows you to start small and grow very large, through linear expandability.

Globally, Teradata covers both the private and public sectors, with over nine hundred customers and more than two thousand implementations. Teradata is well represented across all industries. Teradata is used by all of the top ten largest telecommunications companies, over sixty percent of the largest retailers, airlines, and freight companies, as well as half of the world's largest banks. Teradata Corporation estimates that over a million users each day, access Teradata data warehouses.

The Basic Teradata Database Architecture

Teradata is an RDBMS that manages vast quantities of data. Teradata's strengths are drawn from its massively parallel processing, its ability to handle many simultaneous requests, and its ability to act as a single data store. Teradata architecture is renowned for its exceptional scalability, which allows the system to improve performance by adding additional processors, which in turn allows for more connections and querying.

> *Tip* – Teradata is a Massively Parallel Processing MPP system. It is designed to be highly scalable and flexible to meet your business needs.

This architecture makes Teradata an excellent choice for decision support and business intelligence purposes.

The following diagram illustrates the process flow of a query being submitted to Teradata Database:

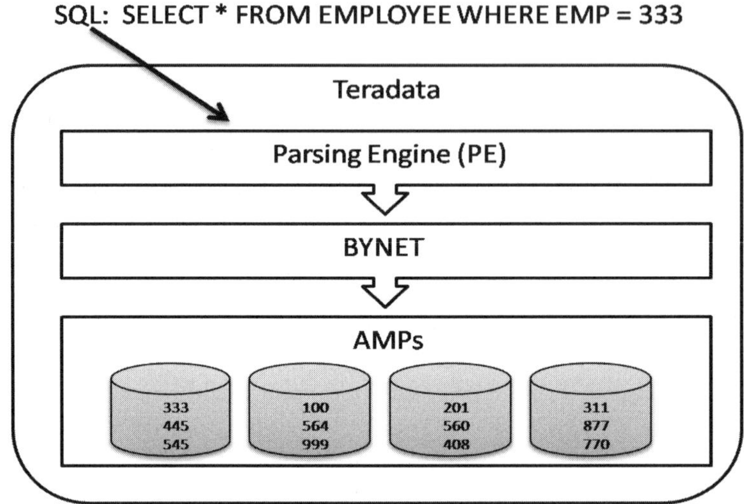

Teradata is unique in the method in which it processes queries. The above, is a high-level illustration of a simple query execution on Teradata. The user's SQL statement is submitted to the Parsing Engine (PE). The PE is responsible for checking the query syntax, verifying the user's security, and formulating the plan for the AMPs. Once completed, the PE communicates with the AMPs across the BYNET. Finally, the AMPs retrieve the necessary data rows to resolve the query.

Parsing Engine

The Parsing Engine's (PE) purpose is to formulate the most efficient and least expensive plan, in order to return the requested response set.

Processing paths are evaluated and the fastest path is chosen as illustrated below.

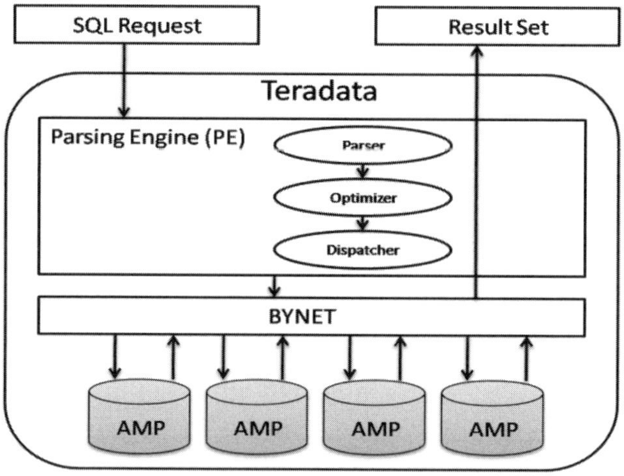

This plan is converted to executable steps, which are performed by the AMPs, and finally passed to the dispatcher.

The PE is also responsible for any necessary input conversions, such as a character set conversion from EBCDIC to ASCII.

As illustrated in the above diagram, for every submitted request, the PE:

1. Verifies the syntax of the request (SQL)
2. Verifies the user's security permissions to determine if the target object (table, views, macros, etc.) can be accessed
3. Parses and optimizes SQL
4. Formulates the execution plan for the AMPs, which entails breaking the process down into a series of steps
5. Returns result answer-set back to the client

Note: the PE can handle up to 120 individual user sessions.

Teradata BYNET

The Parsing Engine does not communicate directly to the AMPs. Instead, a communication pathway, known as the Teradata BYNET®, sits between the AMPs and PEs. The PE transmits the plan to the AMPs via the BYNET. In response, the data that the AMPs retrieve from disks are returned to the PE via the BYNET.

The BYNET is an optimized interconnect system designed for delivering messages between nodes. Each Teradata configuration has two BYNET channels, which serve a dual purpose. First, the two BYNET channels are fault tolerant, which ensure that communication can continue in the event of a failure on one channel. Second, the BYNET provides a high speed internal network for communications. The channels are bi-directional pathways that send and receive data concurrently.

By design, the BYNET is scalable. The BYNET gets larger proportionately to its Teradata system. This ensures that the communication between the AMPs and the PEs never slow down due to an increase in system size.

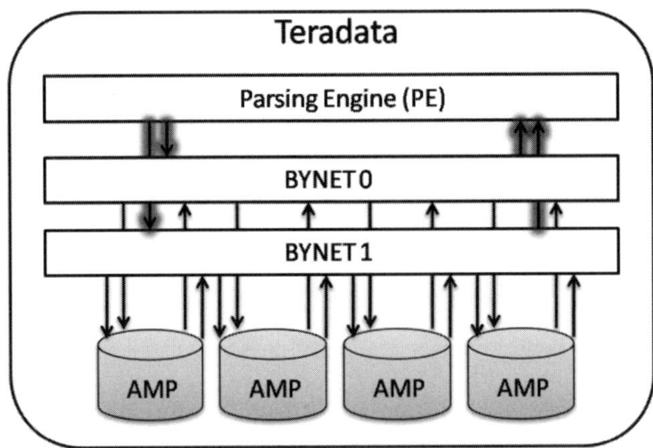

The above diagram demonstrates the sequence of events that occur for every submitted Teradata request:

1. PE validates the submitted request (SQL syntax)
2. PE validates the user's security rights
3. PE determines the execution plan for the AMPs
4. PE submits the plan to the AMPs (via the BYNET)
5. AMPs use the instructions in the plan to retrieve the data
6. AMPs return the data back to the PE (via the BYNET)
7. PE returns the data to the

Access Module Processors

The Access Module Processors (AMPs) perform the physical task of retrieving the result data. In addition, the AMPs perform any necessary output conversions, such as data type conversions. The AMPs connect to a single virtual disk (VDISK), which consists of a number of physical disks (PDISK).

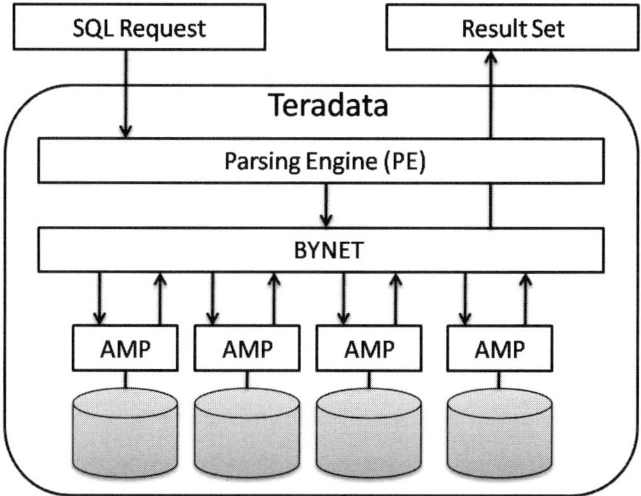

The above illustration reveals how the AMPs fit into the overall process. The rows of each table on a Teradata system are distributed evenly across all the AMPs. Each AMP is responsible for the row retrieval for each table on their disk. When queried, the AMP will return its share of the data. The AMPs work independently and therefore retrieve data concurrently. The AMPs are also responsible for aggregating columns, lock management, sorting rows, join processing, output formatting, disk space management, accounting, recovery processing, and special utility protocols.

Shared Nothing Architecture

Teradata is a "shared nothing" (SN) architecture. Each AMP works independently from the rest of the AMPs. AMPs have their own CPU, memory, and disk. AMPs do not connect directly to other AMPs. Each AMP has a direct connection to the network via the BYNET. AMPs do not rely on each other to complete their individual assignments, nor do they inhibit each other's operations.

As illustrated in the following example, each AMP should have a relatively equal amount of rows from each table.

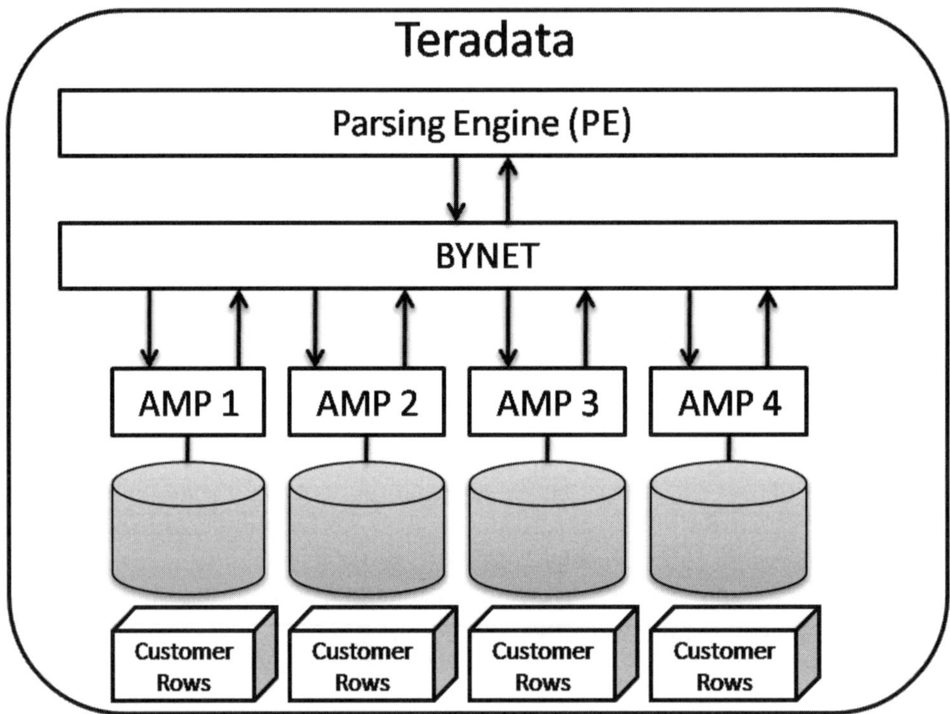

Linear Scalability

The Teradata Database is a "shared nothing, infinitely scalable" system, which means it has the capability to achieve "linear scalability". Linear scalable architectures ensure that performance should improve, and never diminish, as the system resources grow.

In regard to Teradata, linear scalability is achieved by adding more system resources to the configuration. This starts with adding Nodes to the system, which consequently provides additional PEs, BYNET, and disks to the architecture. The new architecture also adds more AMP's as this illustration below demonstrates.

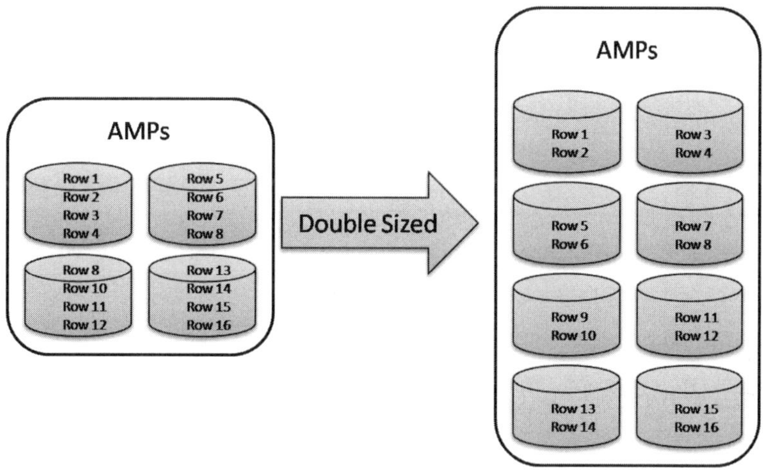

In the above illustration, we doubled the Teradata configuration size by adding system resources to the architecture. As discussed, AMPs will proportionately increase as the system is upgraded. Increasing the system resources by deploying improved node technologies, enhancing the software version, or adding more AMP's we can double the performance of a Teradata system.

By examining this illustration further, we will demonstrate how linear scalability is achieved. Prior to the upgrade, we had four rows per AMP with a total of 16 rows overall. If a user does a SELECT * to retrieve all of these rows, then each AMP will be responsible for returning four rows each. When the system is upgraded to eight AMP's, only two rows will reside on each AMP.

Now, when performing a SELECT *, each AMP will be responsible for only two rows, and each AMP will work less with the same result. Hence, the query results are returned twice as fast. This concept is referred to as "linear scalability".

Why is scalability important? Scalability translates into flexibility and affordability. If a system is scalable, then the system can start small (pay for only what is needed at that moment) and grow according to its needs, without the threat of system degradation. Good data warehouses typically start small and eventually become large centralized Enterprise Data Warehouses (EDW).

Remember, all database systems are different, and most are not designed to be used as a data warehouse solution. When choosing a data warehouse platform, scalability should be considered among the top selection criteria. Proper planning and good decision making will ensure that you're data warehouse can meet the needs of today and tomorrow.

Note: To achieve linear scalability, one must ensure that their data is evenly distributed to take advantage of the performance gain. Data distribution is dictated by the Primary Index column(s), which will be discussed in more detail throughout this book.

Inside a Teradata Cabinet

Teradata refers to each individual server within a system as a *node*. The node is comprised of both hardware and software. Each node has its own operating system (OS), its own copy of the Teradata RDMBS software, its own CPUs, memory, and disk space.

In turn, a Teradata cabinet consists of one or more nodes. A Teradata system can have more than one cabinet.

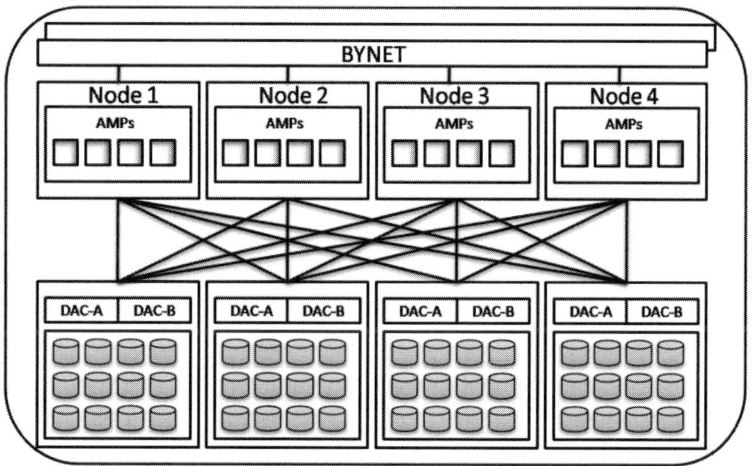

Teradata can run on multiple operating systems, including Novel SUSE Linux (64-bit), Microsoft Windows Server (32-bit on older systems, 64-bit on newer systems), and UNIX MP-RAS (32-bit). Companies usually choose the OS that best fits their organizational design and needs.

Older Teradata systems have between one and two, single core or dual core, processors. Teradata's newer systems offer up to two quad core Intel® Xeon® processors. Depending on the model and OS, each node can have between 4 and 32 GB of memory.

Each node is connected to the BYNET (hardware or software, depending on the platform), which is the communication path for the entire system. The minimum number of nodes in any Teradata system is one. Depending on the Teradata server platform, the maximum number of nodes varies. For example, the Teradata Active

Enterprise Data Warehouse server can support 1,024 nodes, and up to 10,000 terabytes (10 petabytes) of data.

In the diagram on the previous page, we illustrate a four node Teradata system. Each node has two Intel® processors and 32 GB of memory where the AMPs and PEs are configured. Because AMPs and PEs are memory resident, they are referred to as Virtual Processors (VPROCs). The node connects to both the BYNET and to a virtual disk set, which is a set of disks. The virtual disk is where the AMP's share of the table data is physically stored.

Summary

The three most important components of a Teradata system are the Parsing Engine (PE), AMP, and BYNET. These components work together to process a user's request and to access and return the resulting data. Each component has a unique set of tasks, and each component is autonomous from the others.

Teradata's shared nothing architecture ensures that this system will be extremely scalable. A Teradata system's performance will increase proportionately with an increased number of nodes. This concept is called "Linear scalability", which enables you to start with a small, more affordable system, while giving the ability to grow the system as business and data needs increase.

Chapter 2 - The Lazy DBA

Obtaining Knowledge Certifications Standards

The best DBA is the "Lazy" DBA. This does not imply that a DBA should be a slacker, or not respond quickly, or not get his/her job done. On the contrary, this means they should be extremely efficient by using the full technology to their advantage. The more knowledge someone gains and uses, the more valuable they become.

There are many avenues for obtaining knowledge. Take classes, attend the Partners Conference along with regional User Group meetings, and absolutely start studying to get certified. The certification process promotes systematic learning on a broad spectrum of topics that would be arduous to learn otherwise. Teradata Certified Masters are put in an elite group that provides for daily inter-communications with other masters to share information, knowledge, and experiences.

Lastly, it's a good idea to apply for a position on one of the Partner's committees that Teradata supports. These committees consist of the Partners Steering Committee, the Product Advisory Council (PAC), the Service Focus Team (SFT), and the Analytical Applications Product Advisory Council (AAPAC). Learn from other team members, make lifelong contacts, and have access to resources that would be nearly impossible any other way. It's impossible to put a price tag on the benefits from being a Teradata Certified Master or from being a member of one of these committees.

> *Tip* - Apply for a position on one of the Partners committees or teams that Teradata supports, such as the Partners Steering Committee PAC, SFT, and AAPAC.

Automate everything possible by developing proficiency with SQL, Macros, Stored Procedures and dynamic SQL. Most repetitive tasks can be automated to some degree, if not completely. If you haven't already, it is time to stop manually running reports over and over. There are many tools such as Query scheduler, Teradata Manager, Business Intelligence tools, UNIX cron or other schedulers, and even Microsoft schedulers that can help schedule and automate these processes. Considerable time will be invested initially to create automated processes, but this will quickly free up more time later on to enable DBAs to respond efficiently and immediately when requests come in. This is not being lazy at all. This is just plain smart.

Documentation and Communication

In addition to early automation, providing early communication and documentation is also very important. Documenting and publicizing a service catalog for the DBA activities will benefit both the DBA team as well as client organizations. Please see Appendix A for an example of a Development DBA Service Catalog, and Appendix B for an example of a Production DBA Service Catalog. These documents, such as the one found in Appendix A, bring focus to the DBA team. They also provide a checklist to consider during project planning. Client organizations and Managers appreciate these documents because clear expectations are set.

Testing

It is imperative to create a performance benchmark, patch testing, and regression testing process. A proper performance benchmark should be one of the first automation exercises. At a minimum, this process should be run before and after every major and patch upgrade so that there is a baseline to compare relative performance. This process should also be implemented on a scheduled basis so you can measure performance impacts on data volumes, new features, functions, hardware, etc. Benchmarks are discussed in detail in the Performance Benchmark chapter because of their importance.

Extensive regression testing needs to be automated as well because it will be needed for every upgrade, patch application, third-party software upgrade, etc. Minor patch releases have been known to enforce features that were never enforced before in addition to fixing existing defects. This implies the need for diligent and thorough testing every time the system is upgraded. Every event that causes problems or system restarts should be captured and added to the patch test plan or process. It will be a black eye for the DBA group when a patch is backed out of production because it introduced a feature that was not tested prior, and especially if it is caused by a recurrent problem.

Establish Conventions and Standards

It may not be obvious, but simple things like establishing standards and conventions early-on will save tremendous amounts of time and headaches later. For example, implementing naming conventions for databases, tables, columns, etc. will foster the automation of many processes and procedures. Mind you, this is not the only benefit by far. Everyone benefits by naming standards and conventions. Imagine the nightmare when some tables and columns use the word "PARENT" and others use "PRNT" or "PAR". Just writing SQL to accommodate such inconsistencies is difficult enough. These standards should not only be set at the application level, but at the enterprise or corporate level.

It is also important to establish a governance committee at the enterprise level to institute modeling and architecture standards and then to enforce these standards. This committee would be responsible for holding each corporate project accountable to the established standards. The governance committee should be comprised of architects, developers, DBAs, and logical and physical modelers. This will greatly improve the ability for different systems to talk with and play nice with each other. A common vocabulary is priceless when it comes to porting data from source systems to the Enterprise Data Warehouse.

"All generalizations are false, including this one."

Just remember, that guidelines and rules are important, but sometimes it is important not to apply rules globally. For example, someone reads a book and decides to implement surrogate keys or system generated keys. So, a rule is set forth in stone to apply these keys to every table in the system going forward. Is this really a good idea to apply such a rule so globally? There are many ramifications to such a decision, which need to be considered, tested, and weighed out. We are not implying that it is impossible to make it work (depending on the specifics of the situation or application), however; it may require more tables than expected, and definitely more joins. A good buddy once said, "Any rule applied globally and absolutely is absolutely applied wrong!"

Examples of Database Conventions

The following illustrates how rules can be established, and then how simple automation can be used to enforce and report on these rules. These conventions and many more are documented more comprehensively in Appendix C.

- Don't allow any database or object names greater than 25 characters (less is better).

  Notes on Rule: This is a rule that mainly benefits Developers and DBAs for automation and changes. However, it also provides room for suffixes and/or prefixes for index names, constraint names, etc. It's a good idea to keep names concise anyway, but it is imperative that DBAs have the ability to rename objects and append or prefix names with tags. This becomes quite difficult when the tables are already 30 characters long, and now characters have to be dropped off in order to append or prefix them to the name.

- For project-related and for production tables, require names for indexes and establish a naming convention for them.

These rules need to be agreed upon and signed off by a team of architects, DBAs, developers, etc. (e.g. the Governance Committee). Once this is done, the DBA can start automating processes. The following macro validates DDL against the rules mentioned above. The final macro will validate all the rules that are possible to automate. First, create the tables in a test or development database. Then execute the macro as illustrated in the following example.

DDL Validation Macro Example

```
REPLACE MACRO VALIDATE_STANDARDS (DB_IN CHAR(30))
/* This reports on General Naming Standards for a given Database */
AS (

/* Checks Database Names are 25 characters or less. */
SELECT
  d.DatabaseName (Title 'Conflict//DB//Name') (FORMAT 'X(24)'),
  CHAR(TRIM(d.DatabaseName)) (Title 'Length of DBNM > 25')
FROM DBC.DataBases d
WHERE (CHAR(TRIM(d.DatabaseName)) > 25)
      AND d.DatabaseName = :DB_IN
ORDER BY 1;

/* Checks Object Names are 25 characters or less. */
SELECT
   TableName (Title 'Conflict//Object//Name') (FORMAT 'X(24)'),
   DatabaseName (Title 'From Dbase/User') (FORMAT 'X(24)') ,
   CASE TableKind
         WHEN 'T' THEN 'TABLE'
         WHEN 'V' THEN 'VIEW'
         WHEN 'M' THEN 'MACRO'
         WHEN 'P' THEN 'PROCEDURE'
         WHEN 'X' THEN 'TRIGGER'
         WHEN 'J' THEN 'INDEX'
         ELSE TableKind
    END  (Title 'Object Type') (FORMAT 'X(24)'),
    CHAR(TRIM(TableName)) (Title 'Length of TableName > 25')
FROM DBC.Tables
WHERE   (CHAR(TRIM(TableName)) > 25)
      AND DatabaseName = :DB_IN
      AND TableKind NOT IN ('J')
ORDER BY 1;
/* Lists all Tables, Indices etc. with Null Names. */
SELECT DatabaseName, TableName, IndexName,
         IndexType AS "Type", UniqueFlag AS "Unique"
FROM DBC.Indices
WHERE DatabaseName  = :DB_IN
   AND IndexName IS NULL
ORDER BY 1,2,3; );
```

To execute the macro:

```
EXEC VALIDATE_STANDARDS('CSQL_CLASS');
```

The SQL above can be written in a multitude of ways, but this hopefully illustrates how to go about automating the rules that are put in place. Again, a little time invested up-front to develop these validation scripts will have tremendous payoffs down the road. Rules can be instituted, but conflicts are not going to be caught with the human eye. Modeling tools, like ERwin, can be configured to apply many rules, but not all.

We just mentioned a few database-related rules that may apply, but you will need to create your own more comprehensive knowledge book of Data Modeling. This will be required to cover enterprise-wide conventions and guidelines, as well as conceptual, logical and physical designs. It should also cover and detail database standards for different database platforms, a dictionary of terms, abbreviations, class words, reserved words, and so on. The governance committee will be tasked with making sure the rest of the enterprise follows these standards and guidelines, which will probably require regular meetings and reviews.

Backup and Recovery

Every database platform and application needs a well documented and tested plan or strategy for how databases will be backed up and restored in the case of failure. This process should not only meet your business requirements, but also needs to be efficient on both the backup and recovery ends as well. Make sure consensus and sign off is obtained from management so when something goes awry, all parties will be involved in resolving the problem in a timely manner.

Decisions will need to be discussed, agreed upon, and documented for such topics as retention, purge criteria, offsite storage, journaling, fallback, real time verses batch processing, full ALL AMP backups, Cluster Backups, partial or partition backups, backup to disc or tape, backup windows, etc. and how to address each. The actual plan may be a hybrid of some or all of the above and more. A homegrown solution may even meet requirements better.

Real time processing and intraday loads pose a more challenging problem than say monthly batch loaded systems. Do we backup the tables weekly, daily, or more often? If the tables are large enough, do we back up the source files instead, and then how long do we retain these files? Are we receiving incremental changes or full data refreshes? There are many more questions that need to be addressed, but they all need to be handled. Also, there are third-party vendors who may be able to address offsite records storage management, retention, and protection requirements.

Touching on Fallback

First of all, what is Fallback? Fallback provides the automatic recovery from certain failure scenarios, which are mentioned in greater detail below. Fallback manages redundant copies (*"fallback copies"*) of data objects on different storage subsystems within a single database instance, minimizing the impact of major failure scenarios mentioned below.

Make sure management signs off on all decisions. For example, if the decision was made to use or not use Fallback, then management needs to understand the ramifications of this decision, and they need to sign off either way. Fallback utilization is a business decision and needs to be justified by weighing in risk, overhead, cost, and benefit. Although it may be rare, every system is susceptible to an incident that could bring down an AMP, cause data corruption or cause a failure in a particular RAID device. Here are just a few possible failure scenarios.

Fallback Related Failure Scenarios

- It is possible but very rare for both components in a redundant environment to fail. In this case, the subsystem is said to have experienced a *double-fault* (a.k.a., *dual-fault*). Although rare, this is not to say it doesn't happen. An example is when a disc device fails, and then while the redundant device is running in degraded mode waiting for the hot standby to sync up or the original to be replaced, the redundant device also fails.

- It is also rare but possible to encounter an unrecoverable bit error during the reconstruction of a RAID pair. When this occurs, both discs have experienced a fail-fast event, and the I/O subsystem will be rendered unavailable, causing the system to come to a grinding halt. This may require a complete rebuild of the database.

- There are other rare occurrences, such as human error and cabling issues, disc controllers that write corrupted IOs for an hour or so before being detected.

Even though all of these failure scenarios are rare, they are not unique to Teradata. These failures can, and do, occur on any hardware or software system in the industry. The cumulative probability of a failure event occurring in larger systems is significantly higher due to the sheer number of components involved. Excessive down time can be expected for restoring and reconciling tables consisting of hundreds, millions, or even billions of rows. This may have obvious implications to the business at hand.

The DBA needs to make sure that management is fully aware of what's involved in terms of technology, disk requirements, risk, dollars, CPU and IO consumption. In the event of one of these rare but potential failures, management needs to weigh the cost of implementing Fallback verses restoring. Fallback will require twice the storage capacity or twice the disc for those tables we decide to implement Fallback. There will also be implications on IO because each block needs to be written twice resulting in a slight increase in CPU usage to perform these writes.

The architecture and management team(s) may decide that only certain tables deserve such protection or they may decide not to use it at all because the system is small enough and the number of such failures does not merit the cost. Just make sure management is well informed of all the facts, risks, and costs, and get <u>them</u> to make the final business decision. This is not to say that the architecture or DBA teams can not propose a solution either way.

We have just touched on one area of concern -- Fallback. There are many other areas mentioned above that need to be considered and decisions made on. Although there should be an overall strategy for the platform, the backup and restore document needs to be addressed for every new project to make sure the initial plan meets the needs of current requirements, which are continuously evolving.

Teradata is a stable platform, but don't believe those who claim that Teradata is so stable that it doesn't need to be backed up. Teradata would never make this claim, and if anything, erring should be on the side of having too many backups than not enough. Keep abreast of new technology because improvements are constantly being made and your strategies for backup and restores need to be addressed, readdressed, tested, and retested.

Summary

The "Lazy" DBA is really about being anything but lazy. It is about being proactive, efficient, working smarter and gaining knowledge. Through proper automation and utilization of tools, a DBA can make their life so much more pleasant. However, there are some up-front costs because time needs to be invested in education and automation, but the rewards are soon reaped. Eventually, there will be even more time to be proactive for the business.

Efficiency is gained through the establishment of conventions and standards as well. For example, naming conventions are integral to automation. Standards need to be documented, accepted, and communicated across the organization. Decisions need to be agreed upon in areas such as testing, backups, locking techniques, and fallback.

> ***"Ability is like a check, it has no value unless it gets cashed."***

Certifications are not indicative of your effectiveness, or ability, and they are certainly no substitute for real work experience. We strongly encourage the pursuit of certifications, not as a sales pitch, but to foster knowledge and learning. The certification process promotes systematic studying and awareness of topics and features that may otherwise go unrecognized. In addition, achieving the Teradata Master certification allows entry into a privileged group of professionals who share information and consult each other daily. The importance and value of this cannot be emphasized enough.

Chapter 3 - SQL Tips

SQL Tuning
Stats
Skew Identification
Date Calculations

There is no single method or strategy to tune a query. The following discussion will highlight some key areas to focus on. The actual sequence and focus areas are different for every individual, which depends on the maturity of the user community.

This chapter will provide tips and tools for diagnosing and addressing common query flaws. Solutions are provided for certain challenges, and tips are given to improve performance.

We want to emphasize that the most significant query tuning step is to educate users with best practices insight, and Teradata knowledge. Many problems can be resolved by the users if they are given the proper tools beforehand. However, there is a flipside to educating users that is good to be aware of. The more educated a user base gets, the more features they work with. If they utilize new features, DBAs may need to deal with more questions, and potentially, more problems. Knowing the above, it is good practice for continuous learning sessions with all users, especially those new to Teradata.

> *Tip* – Hold continuous learning sessions with all users, especially those new to Teradata.

SQL Tuning

Now let's discuss a strategy and some touch points for tuning a problem query. The first step is to identify and document the problematic query. There are plenty of tools available to help with this. Teradata provides *Teradata Manager*, *Viewpoint*, and *TASM*, and there are some third-party tools that will help significantly as well. Alerts can be set up to page or email DBAs with queries that are breaking certain established rules such as CPU limits, IO limits, parallelism, and much more.

Once the query is captured, the next step is to start documenting everything by doing the following:

1. Create a directory somewhere to store each individual tuning effort and establish a naming convention for the documents.

2. Insert the initial or original query and document any specifics about it. It is a good idea to list the userid, user's name running the query, contact information, rows returned, run time, initial explain plan, etc. All of this information is important because the ultimate goal is to report on the overall impact the tuning effort had at the end.

It's imperative to give the user as much information as possible to understand the query and the problem. Most importantly, this information will likely be used down the road, so the lessons learned here need to make sense when revisited much later.

The effort may take several days and many revisions, so a well documented process will help keep you from losing sight of the original problem.

Getting Started

The SHOW statement will assist in capturing all of the SQL and DDL related to the query in need of tuning. To run this command, simply type in "SHOW" before the SQL statement as illustrated below.

SHOW SQL Example

```
SHOW SELECT * FROM YourView;
```

The first step here is to capture these results and store all the DDL and SQL somewhere in the document. This may be an appendix in the final document, but it needs to be captured first before anything changes.

This is the baseline and starting point that must never get lost and may later get communicated to the user as the baseline or before picture. The tuning effort may incorporate many tuning iterations and take considerable time, so getting back to the beginning easily is imperative.

Statistic Collection Revisited

It's time to start the investigation. Let's start by looking for missing statistics, and be sure to document the statistics that exist as well as any new statistics that end up getting collected. In our Statistics chapter, we detail the importance of statistic collection as well as the process. The importance of statistics for the Teradata optimizer cannot be expressed enough.

> *Tip* – Automate a process to collect statistics on any user tables that are missing stats. This will not help for new tables that are used immediately, but will cut down on the number of times user tables are the culprit for missing statistics.

The optimizer relies on statistics to determine the best access path to the data. Statistics also assist the optimizer in determining how many rows exist in tables being queried and help predict how many rows will qualify for given conditions. Missing or stale statistics might result in the optimizer choosing a suboptimal method of accessing data tables.

If users have the ability to create their own tables in an ad hoc environment, then that is often a good place to start looking. Automate a process to collect statistics on any user tables that are missing stats. This will not help for new tables that are used immediately, but will cut down on the existing user tables, which typically are the culprit for missing statistics.

As discussed in the Statistics chapter of this book, the Teradata Statistic Wizard can help identify statistic candidates on a given workload or on an individual SQL statement. An alternative is to use the following command and perform an Explain after.

```
diagnostic helpstats on for session;
Explain Select ...;
```

This topic is covered elsewhere, but it is important information to introduce here. Statistic suggestions from the command above are displayed at the bottom of the Explain Plan. Typically, the Explain Plan will recommend superfluous combinations of single and multicolumn statistics. Statistic collection is most likely not required on every suggestion, but the single column statistics may be a good place to start testing.

The optimizer will even suggest combinations on Join Indexes that are not even possible. For example, multicolumn statistics cannot be collected on Join Indices, unless a secondary index already exists on those columns. Just be aware that Diagnostic Helpstats will make these suggestions anyway.

Try starting with primary and secondary indexes, Join Indices, join columns, and qualifying columns. Be aware that explain plans can change as underlying table demographics change.

The Explain and Avoidable Product Joins

When analyzing Explain output, desirable phrases are

- "with high confidence"
- "by way of unique primary INDEX"
- "by way of unique index"
- "single-AMP retrieve"
- "of n partitions."

The following observations will lead to improvement opportunities. Look for low or no confidence factors. If a problem is not resolved by collecting appropriate statistics, then start paying attention to product joins, partition elimination, row redistributions, duplication of rows on all AMPs, large estimation times, and indexes that are not used when expected.

It may be a good idea to develop a strategy or sequence for these observations. For example, some may look for undesired product joins first, where others may look for partition elimination first, if underlying tables are partitioned.

Tip - For every N tables being joined, there needs to be N-1 join conditions.

Make sure to use aliases everywhere when they are established.

Product joins are not always problems. However, it's usually very troublesome to see a Cartesian product join, indicated by the phrase "condition of **("(1=1)")**." This is often caused by a missing join condition, missed alias, or mixing aliases. The following example illustrates how mixing aliases with table names results in a product join.

If required, the following command will provide you a more granular explain plan.

```
diagnostic verboseexplain on for session;
Explain Select ...;
```

Mixing Alias Example

```
SELECT e.Emp_no, e.Lname, d.Dept, d.Dname, d.Mgr
FROM Employee_v  e, Department_v  d
WHERE Employee_v.Dept = d.Dept;
```

The Explain Plan shows a product join as such:

employee_table and Spool 3 are joined using a **product join**, with a **join condition of ("(1=1)")**. The result goes into Spool 1 (group_amps), which is built locally on the AMPs.

Take notice that the query above sets an alias of "e" for the Employee_v view. The problem is caused in the WHERE clause where "Employee_v" is referenced again. The optimizer assumes another join to Employee_v again, but there needs to be another join condition if this were true.

For every N tables being joined, there needs to be N-1 join conditions. Anything less will result in at least one product join. Make sure to use aliases everywhere when they are established. The query above is easily fixed with the following WHERE clause:

```
WHERE e.Dept = d.Dept;
```

The following query will result in a similar product join as the previous problem query.

Missing Join Condition Example

```
SELECT e.Emp_no, e.Lname
FROM Employee_v  e
WHERE Department_v.Dept = 100;
```

This peculiar query is not only missing the join condition, but it's also missing the view reference in the FROM clause. Teradata will assume a join to the Department_v view is desired in this example because it is referenced in the WHERE clause. This is fine as long as the proper join clause is specified as such:

```
WHERE e.Dept = Department_v.Dept;
```

This will get rid of the Cartesian Join indicated by "(1=1)", but may still perform a product join if it will be faster to perform a primary index lookup where Dept = 100 first and Cartesian the single row to the Employee_v underlying table. Specifying the proper join conditions get rid of the Cartesian products.

Table Skewing

The Teradata architecture does leave itself susceptible to skewed tables and even skewed processing, for which both should be avoided. Skewed tables can be avoided by making sure the primary index is well distributed. This does not just occur in permanent tables.

It is common for users to create temporary and volatile tables with badly chosen primary indexes as well. Actually, the most common problem results when someone creates a permanent or even volatile table as a select from a sub-query without specifying a proper primary index.

We strongly suggest making it a standard to always specify the primary index, especially for create-table-as-select statements. Teradata will choose the first column of a select list for the primary index, which may or may not be a good candidate.

Imagine this extreme example. A user creates a table as selecting a gender code as the first column in his select list from a very large table. Gender codes have very few values and will definitely skew a table if left as the primary index. It is likely that this table will run out of space by filling up one AMP before it is fully loaded.

If the primary index is not specified, then make sure the first column chosen is as unique as possible to avoid any problems. First of all, the entire system is affected because it takes a lot of resources and time to load such a table to one or a few AMPs.

Most likely, queries and joins to this new skewed table will also suffer greatly from poor performance. Lastly, the entire database will likely be skewed at the AMP level as well, which affects other users of that database. The figure below depicts a highly skewed 4-AMP system. Because the first AMP is nearly full, it's only a matter of time before errors are received for no more space in the database.

Identifying the Problem

It may surprise some people that a database could read only 15% full, but be impossible to create another empty table or even load another row to any table in that database. Table skewing should be the first place to look. It's caused by an entire AMP or small group of AMPs completely filling up, leaving the rest barely occupied.

The easiest way to identify table skew is through the Teradata Administrator tool. Just right-click on the problem database, select Table Space, sort by SkewFact in descending order, and look for the highest skewed tables of any significant size. Tiny tables may be inherently skewed, so don't worry about them.

Also, by right-clicking on a table and checking the Space by AMP in Teradata Administrator, table skew can be visualized by the Vproc distribution. Sort the results by the CurrentPerm in descending order to see the worst offending Vprocs first.

SQL to Identify Table Skew

If Teradata Administrator is not an option or not preferred, then the following SQL will help identify what tables to start assessing first.

```
LOCK DBC.TableSize FOR ACCESS
SELECT TableName,
SUM(CurrentPerm) AS CurrentPerm,
SUM(PeakPerm) AS PeakPerm,
(100 - (AVG(CurrentPerm) /
        MAX(CurrentPerm)*100)) AS SkewFactor
FROM DBC.TableSize
WHERE DatabaseName=('target database' (CHAR(30)))(NOT CS)
GROUP BY 1
HAVING SkewFactor >= 90
AND SUM(CurrentPerm) > 1000000
ORDER BY SkewFactor DESC;
```

Take note that this example excludes all SkewFactors less than 90 and all tables less than about 1 MB. This is a starting point and it's different for every system. Be sure to adjust these numbers accordingly. The main point is to start with the largest skewed tables with any significant size.

SQL to Identify Database Skew and Capacity

Keep an eye out for databases becoming filled or skewed. The following SQL will help.

```
LOCK DBC.DiskSpace FOR ACCESS
SELECT DatabaseName,
Vproc,
CurrentPerm,
MaxPerm,
(CurrentPerm/MaxPerm)*100 AS VprocPctFull,
SUM(CurrentPerm) OVER (PARTITION BY  DatabaseName) AS DBSize,
(100 - (AVG(CurrentPerm) OVER (PARTITION BY  DatabaseName) /
        MAX(CurrentPerm) OVER (PARTITION BY  DatabaseName)*100)) AS
DBSkewFactor
FROM DBC.DiskSpace
WHERE DatabaseName= ('target database' (CHAR(30)))(NOT CS)
ORDER  BY CurrentPerm DESC;
```

Fixing Skew

Remember, as long as one AMP is full for a given database, then the whole database is full. The database skew is important, but the Vproc percent full is even more important. If any of the Vprocs have a high VprocPctFull, then the entire database is full. If one or a few of the Vprocs read full and none of the others do, then this database is also skewed. A single table could be causing the whole problem.

Tip: It may be best in this circumstance to drop and recreate the table using corrected DDL rather than relying on CREATE-TABLE-AS statements, which drop secondary indices whenever just the primary index is specified in a create table statement.

For well distributed tables, the current perm of each VPROC should nearly equate to the average. So how does this problem get fixed? For a DBA with access to additional space, this is a trivial exercise. Simply, recreate the table to another database with a proper well-distributed primary index. Then the original table can be dropped and recreated with the corrected primary index.

Here is an alternative if there is enough spool space available. Create a volatile table with data and a better primary index. Don't forget to include the "ON COMMIT PRESERVE ROWS" clause, and check the row count. Drop and recreate the original table with the new primary index, and reinsert the data from the volatile table.

Change Primary Index Example

The following examples illustrate how to create the interim tables with the new primary index.

```
CREATE TABLE CSQL_CLASS.Customer_table2 AS
CSQL_CLASS.Customer_table WITH DATA
PRIMARY INDEX ( Customer_name );

or

CREATE VOLATILE TABLE Customer_V AS
CSQL_CLASS.Customer_table WITH DATA
PRIMARY INDEX ( Customer_name )
ON COMMIT PRESERVE ROWS;

-- Check count
SELECT COUNT(*) FROM Customer_V;
```

If additional database space or adequate spool space is not available, then other tables need to be dropped, or the problem table needs to be dropped and recreated with the improved primary index.

Additional SQL Tuning Tips

- Try using GROUP BY all selected columns instead of DISTINCT. We suggest trying both methods to be sure, but if defaulting to one, choose the GROUP BY clause. There is a general rule that GROUP BY - works better for very non-unique sets of data, but in the worst case, GROUP BY still works pretty well either way. We have experienced queries running out of spool or taking painfully long with DISTINCT, especially on very non-unique sets of data. These same queries ran in seconds when converted to GROUP BY.

- Use TOP N instead of Sample N for retrieving sample data quickly. TOP N will quickly retrieve a small sample of data without performing a full table scan. If the ORDER BY clause is excluded, then TOP N will return **any** N base table rows from the system. The ORDER BY clause ensures that the top N rows will be returned according to the order. The good news is that Teradata 13.0 should remove the disparity between these two methods.

- It is also suggested that TOP N is used instead of qualifying ROW_NUMBER or RANK. The worst that TOP N will perform will at least be equivalent to these two functions.

- Try using new OLAP functions like ROW_NUM instead of CSUM. Dramatic performance gains can be made with this conversion. A common practice of the past has been to use **CSUM(1,1)** to generate a sequential number to use as a primary index or row number. Try using **ROW_NUMBER() OVER (ORDER BY 1)** instead.

- Avoid using functions in join conditions. This will require that tables are designed accordingly, by avoiding certain techniques such as intelligent columns. An intelligent column is any column that has more than one piece of information in the column. An example may be concatenating a social security number (SSN) and another code to make another identifier field. The problem truly presents itself when trying to substring this field for use in a join condition. For example, the SSN is parsed out with the SUBSTR function and joined to a social security table on the SSN. The optimizer can make no use of statistics in this case, and thus performance is stymied. If these fields are physically separated, then statistics can be collected, indexes can be created, and the optimizer is no longer hindered.

Date Calculations

It is a good idea to develop a matrix of date techniques and keep it handy. This should be kept readily available so that things like the first or last day of the month, day of the week, ages, etc. can be quickly figured out. Not all of these techniques are as straight-forward as one might think they should be.

We will start with the seemingly easy AGE-in-years calculation, which is very commonly miscalculated. Forget about dividing by 365 or 365.25 like other RDBMS professionals suggest. Please be careful with this one because there is a lot of documentation floating around with different ways to calculate this seemingly easy math problem. However, most of them are not 100% correct, and speaking from experience, it is easy to be bitten by this one.

Incorrect Age Calculations

Before giving the correct answer, we will illustrate a few more common mistakes that give a right answer **most** of the time. To say any of these work most of the time, really means they are the wrong solution. We want the reader to identify and avoid these incorrect methods. Here are three commonly misused methods for calculating age in Teradata.

```
Wrong Age 1 = (CALENDAR_DATE - DATE '1928-10-16') YEAR(4)

Wrong Age 2 = CAST((( CALENDAR_DATE - DATE '1928-10-16')
              MONTH(4) ) AS INTERVAL YEAR(4))

Wrong Age 3 = (CALENDAR_DATE - DATE '1928-10-16')/365
```

WARNING! The AGE calculations mentioned above are all fairly close, but none of them are 100% accurate, so please try and avoid all of these methods. We only mentioned these methods so that they will be easily identified and corrected if used anywhere. If close is good enough, then go for it.

Correct Age Calculation

The following method may not be so intuitive, but the important thing is that it is correct. The correct AGE is calculated by taking the difference of the integer values between two dates and dividing them by 10,000.

```
Correct Age = (CAST(CALENDAR_DATE  AS INT) - CAST(DATE '1928-10-16' AS INT)) / 10000
```

Testing Age Calculations

Test these competing methods by performing the following test. Here we calculate the various ages for a person born October 16, 1928. The results are wrong even within the first year, but it takes a few years before even BAD_AGE3 is wrong, even though it's the closest.

```
SEL CALENDAR_DATE,
(CAST(CALENDAR_DATE  AS INT) - CAST(DATE '1928-10-16' AS INT)) / 10000 AS
RIGHT_AGE,
(CALENDAR_DATE - DATE '1928-10-16') YEAR(4) AS BAD_AGE1,
CAST(((CALENDAR_DATE - DATE '1928-10-16') MONTH(4) ) AS INTERVAL YEAR(4)) AS
BAD_AGE2,
(CALENDAR_DATE - DATE '1928-10-16')/365  AS BAD_AGE3
FROM SYS_CALENDAR.CALENDAR
WHERE EXTRACT (YEAR FROM CALENDAR_DATE) > 1927
AND  EXTRACT (DAY FROM CALENDAR_DATE) IN (1,2,15,16,17,27,28,29,30,31)
ORDER BY 1;
```

Ouput

CAL_DATE	RIGHT_AGE	BAD_AGE1	BAD_AGE2	BAD_AGE3
9/29/1932	3	4	3	3
9/30/1932	3	4	3	3
10/1/1932	3	4	4	3
10/2/1932	3	4	4	3
10/15/1932	3	4	4	4
10/16/1932	4	4	4	4
10/17/1932	4	4	4	4

The SQL above chooses days from the beginning, middle and end of each month. This covers days before each birth date, the beginning of each month, and several days to cover leap year and the end of each month. When running this test, mistakes can be identified as early as the first year in the first two BAD methods. In the results above, it is apparent that all three BAD methods produce incorrect results on October 15, 1932. However, the division-by-10,000 method works every time by changing only on the October 16th birth date.

Special Note: Some of the following examples utilize ODBC Scalar Functions (i.e. DAYOFMONTH, DAYOFWEEK, etc.) that can only be called via an ODBC connection. These will not work from BTEQ, and you can't create views that use them, unfortunately.

Different Ways to Return the Day of the Week

The rest of this section sites other popular date tips without quite so much elaboration. There are sometimes different ways to get the same result.

```
SEL CAST(CAST(DATE AS FORMAT'E4') AS CHAR(9));

SEL DATE (FORMAT 'EEEE') (CHAR(9));

Answer:  Saturday      (Both return long version of the day)


SEL DATE (FORMAT 'E3') (CHAR(9));

Answer:  Sat      (Returns short version of the day)
```

If one prefers to write a lot of code, then the CALENDAR view can always be queried as such:

```
SEL
CASE
   WHEN DAY_OF_WEEK = 1 THEN 'Sunday'
   WHEN DAY_OF_WEEK = 2 THEN 'Monday'
   WHEN DAY_OF_WEEK = 3 THEN 'Tuesday'
   WHEN DAY_OF_WEEK = 4 THEN 'Wednesday'
   WHEN DAY_OF_WEEK = 5 THEN 'Thursday'
   WHEN DAY_OF_WEEK = 6 THEN 'Friday'
   WHEN DAY_OF_WEEK = 7 THEN 'Saturday'
ELSE 'What?'
END AS "WEEK DAY NAME"
FROM SYS_CALENDAR.CALENDAR
WHERE CALENDAR_DATE=DATE;
```

Other Date formatting Examples

```
SEL DATE (FORMAT 'E4,BM4BDD,BY4') (VARCHAR(35));

Answer:  Saturday, July 18, 2009

SEL DATE (FORMAT 'YYYY-MM-DD') (CHAR(10));

Answer:  2009-07-18

SEL EXTRACT (MONTH FROM DATE),
    EXTRACT (DAY FROM DATE),
    EXTRACT (YEAR FROM DATE);

Answer: 7        18        2009
```

This produces the same result:

```
SEL MONTH(DATE),
    DAYOFMONTH(DATE),        -- ODBC Scalar Function
        YEAR(DATE);

Answer: 7        18        2009
```

Other Common Date Calculations

- These all calculate the previous end of the month

```
SEL DATE - (DATE MOD 100);

SEL DATE - EXTRACT(DAY FROM  DATE);

SEL DATE - DAYOFMONTH(DATE);

SEL DATE '2009-07-18'  - EXTRACT(DAY FROM  DATE '2009-07-18' );

Answer:  2009-06-30
```

- These calculate the end of the month

```
SEL ADD_MONTHS(DATE,1) –
EXTRACT (DAY FROM ADD_MONTHS(DATE,1));

SEL ADD_MONTHS(DATE,1) -
DAYOFMONTH(ADD_MONTHS(DATE,1));

SEL ADD_MONTHS(DATE '2009-07-18',1) -
DAYOFMONTH(ADD_MONTHS(DATE '2009-07-18',1));

Answer:  2009-06-30
```

- This calculates the first of any year

```
SEL  DATE - DAYOFYEAR(DATE) + 1;

SEL DATE - CAST(CAST((DATE (FORMAT 'DDD'))  AS
VARCHAR(3)) AS INT) +1;

Answer:  2009-01-01
```

- This calculates the last of any year

```
SEL  DATE - DAYOFYEAR(DATE) + INTERVAL '1' YEAR;

SEL DATE - CAST(CAST((DATE (FORMAT 'DDD'))  AS
VARCHAR(3)) AS INT) + INTERVAL '1' YEAR;

Answer:  2009-12-31
```

- These calculate the first of the month

```
SEL (DATE - DATE MOD 100) + 1

SEL (DATE - EXTRACT(DAY FROM  DATE))+1;

SEL (DATE - DAYOFMONTH(DATE)) + 1;

SEL (DATE '2009-07-18' - DATE '2009-07-18' MOD 100) + 1;

Answer:  2009-07-01
```

- Returns the quarter begin date

```
SEL CAST( DATE/10000*10000 + (EXTRACT(MONTH FROM
DATE)-1)/3*300+101 AS  DATE);

SEL CAST( DATE/10000*10000 + (MONTH(DATE)-1)/3 * 300 +
101 AS  DATE);

SEL CAST( DATE '2009-07-18'/10000*10000 +
(EXTRACT(MONTH FROM DATE '2009-07-18')-1)/3*300+101 AS
DATE );

Answer:  2009-07-01
```

- This returns the quarter end date

```
SEL ADD_MONTHS(CAST(DATE/10000*10000 + (EXTRACT
(MONTH FROM DATE)-1)/3*300+101 AS DATE),3  )-1;

SEL ADD_MONTHS(CAST(DATE/10000*10000+(MONTH (DATE) -
1)/3*300+101 AS DATE),3 )-1;

SEL ADD_MONTHS(CAST(DATE '2009-07-18'/10000 *10000 +
(EXTRACT(MONTH FROM DATE '2009-07-18')-1)/3*300+101 AS
DATE ),3)-1;

Answer:  2009-09-30
```

- This returns the quarter

```
SEL QUARTER(DATE);

Answer:  3
```

Be sure to test every possibility as we did earlier for the AGE calculations.

Testing Any Date Calculations

The following example shows how to test the various possibilities by selecting every possible CALENDAR_DATE value from SYS_CALENDAR.CALENDAR.

```
SEL CALENDAR_DATE,
    (CALENDAR_DATE - CALENDAR_DATE MOD 100) + 1,
    (CALENDAR_DATE - EXTRACT(DAY FROM  CALENDAR_DATE))+1,
    (CALENDAR_DATE - DAYOFMONTH(CALENDAR_DATE)) + 1
FROM SYS_CALENDAR.CALENDAR
WHERE EXTRACT (YEAR FROM CALENDAR_DATE) > 1927
ORDER BY 1;
```

There are obviously many more date calculations that can be made, and these examples should illustrate that they are not all too intuitive. That is why we suggest that making a list or a matrix of the various possibilities, and keep it readily available. These are great for training the user community as well. They may come up with more in the process. Just make sure to test everything as thoroughly as possible. It's a good idea to test these calculations before and after upgrades and patches as well.

Summary

SQL tuning is not an exact science and it takes years to master, if it can be mastered. It is best to have a plan or strategy, and systematically attack each and every problem the same way every time. Document every finding as a lesson learned so that the wheel doesn't have to be reinvented every time. Remember, the most important factor in SQL tuning is self-education and education for all users. The real trick is to have users tune their own queries.

Chapter 4 - Join Types and Strategies

Join Types
Join Strategies
Explained

The best way to access data in Teradata is by using the Primary Index, followed by Secondary Indexes. However, once we begin joining two or more tables together, queries become more complicated, and proper joining is critical. We need to utilize some best practices to ensure that we are accessing the data as efficiently and effectively as possible. Poorly written joins can be costly in terms of response time and performance, as well as the time spent writing the wrong query.

A join occurs whenever the rows of two or more tables are combined, based upon a common column between the tables. Currently, Teradata can join up to 64 tables in a single SQL statement (and soon it will be 128). The joins originate from the user's query, and can be inner, outer (left, right, and full), exclusion, cross, Cartesian, or self joins.

The Teradata optimizer analyzes the query and determines the best path or join strategy for the query. The join constraint (WHERE or ON clause) in the user's query provides the optimizer with clues on what to do. Although the user can help influence the type of join that Teradata might choose, the optimizer is the definitive authority.

This chapter will focus on the different joins strategies that Teradata utilizes to access data. The goal of this chapter is to provide you with an understanding of how Teradata joins tables and the performance implications of each join strategy.

Basic Join Example

The following illustration shows an Employee and Department table. If we want to get the name of the department for each employee, we must join the two tables together.

Employee Table

EMP (UPI)	DEPT	LNAME	FNAME	SALARY
258	50	Jackson	Jane	55000
369	22	Rogers	John	65000
963	22	Gains	George	60000

Department Table

DEPT (UPI)	DEPT_NAME
14	Sales
22	Marketing
35	Support

Upon inspection, we can determine that both tables have a DEPT column. The DEPT column will serve as our join column. The below SQL demonstrates how we would join the tables together.

```
SELECT
            E.EMP
           ,E.LNAME
           ,D.DEPT_NAME
FROM  EMPLOYEE as E
INNER JOIN  DEPARTMENT as D
ON       E.DEPT = D.DEPT;
```

Join Types:

The optimizer will analyze the user's query and review the join types within the query. Upon conclusion of the review, the optimizer will choose the best join plan (by selecting a join strategy) for the query and execute the request.

For the sake of review, let's briefly discuss the different types of joins that can be written in SQL:

- **Inner Join:** Returns the matched rows from both tables. No unmatched rows are returned.
- **Left Outer:** Returns the matched rows from both tables. Also returns any unmatched rows from table on the left side of the join.
- **Right Outer:** Returns the matched rows from both tables. Also returns any unmatched rows from table on the right side of the join.
- **Full Outer:** Returns both the matched and unmatched rows from both tables.
- **Self Join:** Compares rows inside the table against other rows inside the exact same table.
- **Cartesian Join:** Compares each row in the first table to each row of the second table, resulting in the return of all rows in the first table multiplied by the number of rows in the second table.

Join Strategies:

The following is a list of join strategies which the optimizer will choose from:

- Merge Join
- Nested Join
- Hash Join
- Exclusion Join
- Inclusion Join
- Product Join
- Cartesian Join

Join Strategies: Merge

A Merge Join will join two rows together, when they are on the same AMP based on an equality join condition. Although this seems simple enough, recall that Teradata distributes a table's data across all of its AMPs. In addition, AMPs store data for multiple tables, whose data is also spread out across the AMPs. In order for a merge join to occur, the data needs to physically reside on the same AMP. Otherwise, redistribution of the data will be required, in order to complete the merge join. Redistribution of data occurs in Spool space.

When two tables join (using a WHERE or ON clause) on their Primary Index (PI) column(s), and if the Primary Index is the exact same column(s) on both tables, then the merge join can be performed because all data resides on the same AMP. In this case, no redistribution of data is required. In situations where non-PI column values are joined, redistribution of data is required in order to complete the request.

In order to perform a merge join, Teradata has four options to choose from. Known as Distribution Strategies, these help Teradata decide the best way to accomplish the merge join.

1. If the primary indexes are the same, it can avoid redistribution, and perform the join right away on the same AMP.
2. Redistribute one of the tables.
3. Redistribute both of the tables.
4. Create a copy of the smaller table on each AMP.

Next, we will discuss each of these steps, in detail.

Join Strategies: Merge Strategy #1

The first merge strategy is to use the Primary Index on both tables to complete the join. This strategy can only be utilized if the join columns and Primary Index columns (or Partitioned Primary Indexes) are the same on both tables within the join as the illustration below depicts.

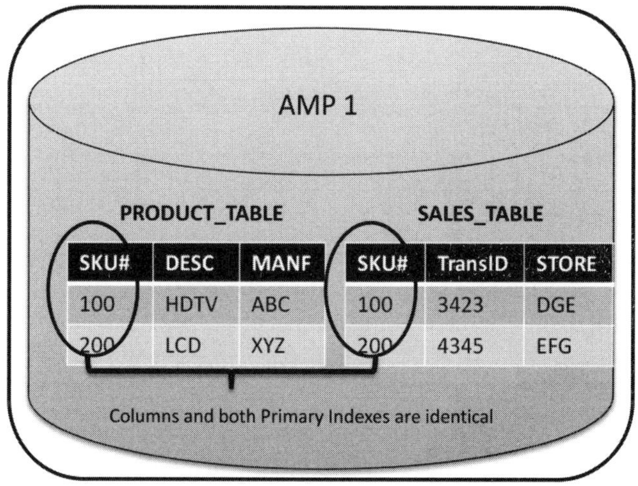

In this case, no Spool space is required, since the data resides on the same AMPs. No redistribution is necessary since the join is AMP local. Teradata will perform a merge join using a row hash match scan. This is the fastest type of join, since no data needs to be moved.

The following SQL statement performs an INNER JOIN on the column SKU# for tables TABLE_A and TABLE_B. Both tables have SKU# defined as their Primary Index:

```
SELECT A.SKU#, A.DESC, B.SKU#, B.TransID
FROM
Product_Table A
INNER JOIN
Sales_Table B
ON A.SKU# = B.SKU#;
```

The join in our example above is AMP local because no data needed to be moved in order to complete the join.

Join Strategies: Merge Strategy #2

If the first merge strategy cannot be utilized, Teradata will attempt to perform the next best type of merge. This merge strategy can be utilized if one of the join columns is a Primary Index and the other join column is a non-indexed column.

In this strategy, data must be redistributed. Teradata has a few redistribution options to consider. First, it can duplicate the entire smaller table on all AMPs. Second, it can leave the table that is using the Primary Index column alone and move the rows from the non-indexed column's table in Spool space.

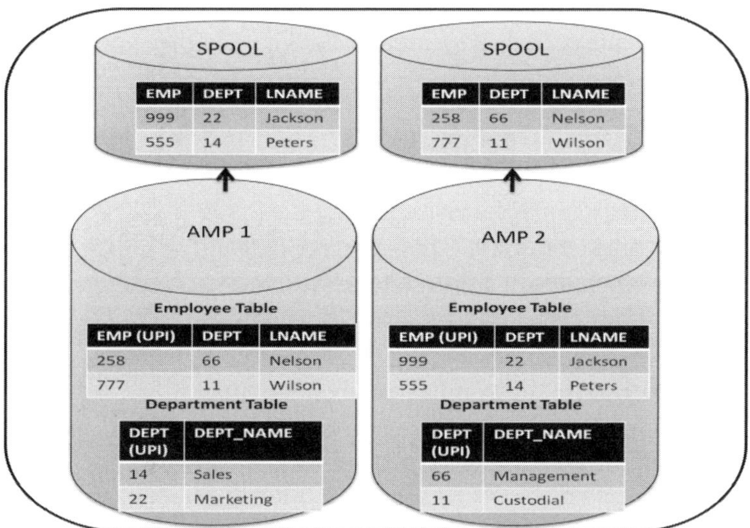

In this case as the illustration shows, the data from Employee Table is moved and hashed to the same AMP based on the Dept number because of the ON clause on the join operation. This strategy is chosen because the Primary Index (PI) on the Department Table.

The following SQL example illustrates the merge strategy. The purpose of the query is to return all employees, along with their department name:

```
SELECT  E.EMP, E.DETP, E.LNAME,
D.DEPT_NAME
FROM EMPLOYEE as E
INNER JOIN
DEPARTMENT as D
ON E.DEPT = D.DEPT;
```

Again notice how the Employee data is moved into the Spool of the AMP where the corresponding Department data is located.

Join Strategies: Merge Strategy #3

Our next merge strategy is implemented if the first two strategies cannot be implemented. This strategy is used when the join is performed on neither table's Primary Index column. In this strategy, the data from both tables is redistributed into Spool and sorted by hash code. Because data from both tables must be hashed and redistributed, this process is both time-consuming and inefficient.

Tip – If you collect stats on the column(s) of the smaller table that are used in the WHERE and ON clauses, you can get a better join plan.

In order to redistribute the data, the values of the non-indexed columns are hashed. Based on their hash value, they are placed on the corresponding AMP.

Once all data is moved to the Spool on their appropriate AMPs, the rows will be physically joined as this diagram shows.

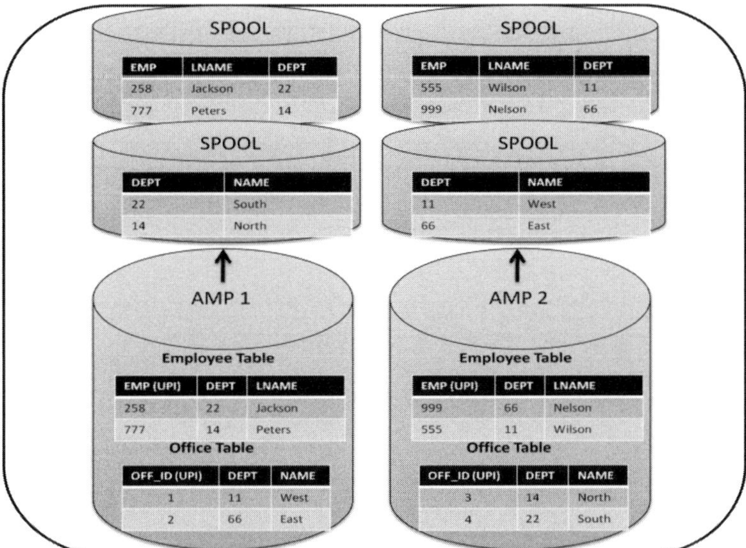

The following SQL example illustrates this particular merge strategy. The purpose of the query is to return the office name for all employees in the Employee table. Office name is stored on the Office table:

```
SELECT E.EMP, E.LNAME, E.DEPT, O.NAME
FROM   EMPLOYEE as E
INNER JOIN
OFFICE as O
ON E.DEPT = O.DEPT;
```

In our example, notice that the data has been moved into Spool on both AMPs 1 and 2. The data was placed in those AMPs according to the hashed values of DEPT, which are the non-indexed join columns for both tables.

Join Strategies: Merge Strategy #4

Our final merge strategy is implemented whenever Teradata determines that it will be more effective than other strategies. Specifically, this strategy is applicable only for PI to non-PI, and non-PI to non-PI column joins. This strategy is only implemented when Teradata determines that one of the joined tables is small enough to justify utilizing the strategy. In this strategy, Teradata will take the smallest table in the join and duplicate it across all of the AMPs as the illustrations demonstrates below. When utilized, this strategy has the potential to be very efficient.

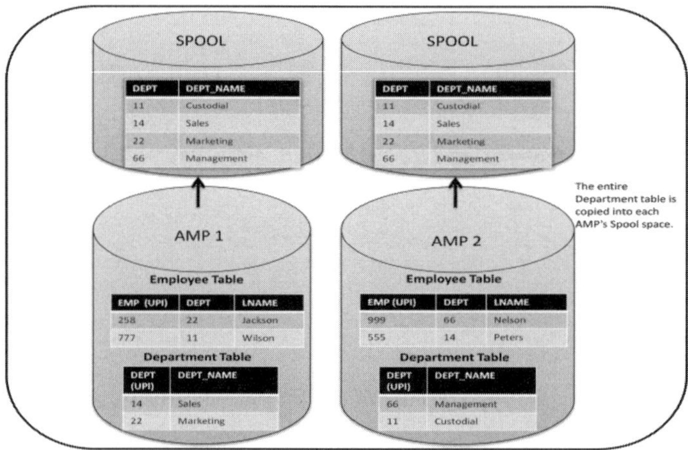

When Teradata determines that the table is sufficiently small in size, it will create a copy of the table within the Spool space on each AMP. After the table has been copied to all AMPs, the join can easily be completed, because the data for both tables co-exist on each AMP.

Note: Collecting statistics on the columns of tables being joined will help influence the join strategy. This is because the optimizer will have better insight on the tables being joined (i.e. small tables vs. large tables).

The following SQL example illustrates this final merge strategy. The purpose of the query is to return all employees, along with their department name.

```
SELECT E.EMP, E.LNAME, D.DEPT_NAME FROM
EMPLOYEE as E
INNER JOIN
DEPARTMENT as D
ON E.DEPT = D.DEPT;
```

Nested Join

There are two types of nested joins. First, a remote Nested Join is a type of join that utilizes either a Unique Primary Index or Unique Secondary Index from the one of the join columns in order to retrieve a single row. Using this type of join requires a WHERE clause, with the indexed column's value set equal to a particular value, in order to limit the data to a single row.

The following SQL example illustrates the Nested Join. The purpose of the query is to return all employees in department number 14, along with the department name:

```
SELECT E.EMP, E.LNAME, D.DEPT_NAME
FROM   EMPLOYEE as E
INNER JOIN
DEPARTMENT as D
ON E.DEPT = D.DEPT
WHERE D.DEPT = 14;
```

Once the WHERE clause targeted row is located on its AMP, Teradata will move the row data to Spool, on each AMP as the illustration depicts.

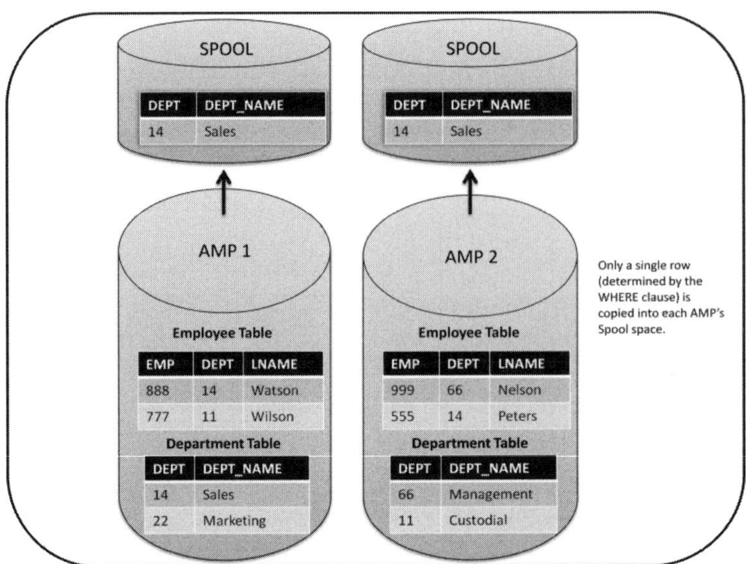

This approach is extremely efficient because Teradata can easily find the WHERE clause information, since it is indexed, and because it only has to redistribute a single row across all AMPs. Once the row has been redistributed into all AMPs Spool space, the joins can complete and the data can be returned.

The second kind of nested join is called local nested join. This join utilizes a secondary index, which can be a USI or NUSI (SI), on one of the join columns. This applies for inner joins and outer joins with equality join conditions.

This join is done in 2 steps. In the first step, the table with the non-indexed column is joined with an SI column. When this occurs, a spool file will be used to store the RowIDs of the qualified rows from the SI's base table. In the second step, the RowIDs in spool are joined with the base table to produce the final result set.

Local nested joins can be effective for non-PI to non-PI column joins where one table is small or has a very selective condition that qualifies a small number of rows from the table, and the other table is large. This join strategy avoids data movement and spooling of the larger table. In addition, it will only retrieve the data blocks required that contain the qualified rows for the join to complete.

Hash Join

The Hash Join is a type of merge join that relies upon an equality condition (i.e. D.DEPT = E.DEPT) where the join columns are similar.

A Hash Join is performed inside of an AMP's memory, rather than Spool. Disk operations are always more time intensive than memory operations because they require many physical read/write operations (which memory does not have to perform) as the picture shows.

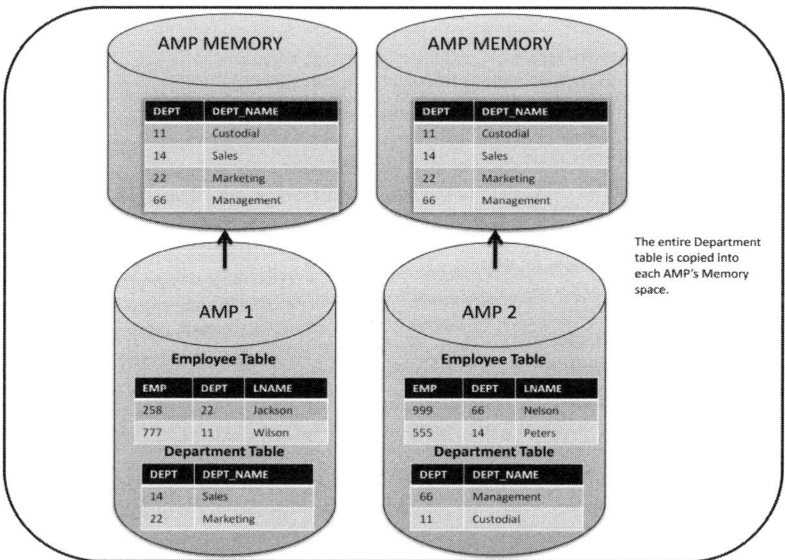

Note: Currently, Hash joins only support self and inner merge join operations based on an equality condition. Support for other join types is planned for future releases.

The following SQL example illustrates the Hash Join. The purpose of the query is to return all employees along with their department name:

```
SELECT E.EMP, E.LNAME, D.DEPT_NAME
FROM EMPLOYEE as E
INNER JOIN DEPARTMENT as D
ON E.DEPT = D.DEPT;
```

A Hash Join can only be performed if one or both of the join tables can fit into the AMP's memory.

The AMP will always try to fit the smallest table into memory. Once the table has been selected for memory insertion, the join column value of the smaller table will be hashed and sorted. The column from the larger table will then be used to perform the match against the rows of the smaller table, which are stored in the AMP's memory. The Hash Join is completed quickly because the larger table does not need to be sorted or redistributed into Spool (which requires disk activity).

When neither of the join tables can fit into the AMP's memory, a hash join can still be used. In this case, the optimizer will spool both tables first and redistribute or duplicate the data based on the locality requirement. Afterwards, the rows in each spool are organized into partitions with each partition containing rows of a certain range of hash codes. Finally, a hash join is then done for one partition from each of the join tables.

Exclusion Join

An Exclusion Join is either a merge or product join strategy. They are utilized when trying to discover what rows do NOT match with a row in another table. Unlike the other joins we have discussed, the purpose of an exclusion join is to prevent certain data from returning. Teradata is looking for the rows in the first table that are NOT IN the other table. Exclusion Joins can only be used if the following operators are used in the query: NOT IN, EXCEPT, or MINUS.

The following SQL example illustrates the Exclusion Join. The purpose of the query is to return all employees in department 14 that are not a manager:

```
SELECT EMP, LNAME
FROM EMPLOYEE
WHERE  E.DEPT = 14
AND EMP NOT IN
    (SELECT MGR_EMP
     FROM DEPARTMENT
     WHERE  MGR_EMP IS NOT NULL);
```

In order to fully compare each row against the exclusion value, the Exclusion Join will always result in a Full Table Scan. Matching rows are eliminated from the ultimate result set. A common mistake when attempting an Exclusion Join is the failure to exclude NULL values. In addition to specifying "NOT IN", you must also specify "AND [COLUMN NAME] IS NOT NULL". Otherwise, records with NULL values will be returned, and you will have unexpected results. Of course, if the join column has a specified column constraint of "NOT NULL", you have nothing to worry about, since NULLs are not possible.

Teradata tests each row to determine if it qualifies for the result set. Any matches found between the two tables will disqualify the row. In addition, any unknowns will disqualify a row. Rows that do not match, qualify for the ultimate result set.

Product Joins

A Product Join compares each row in one table with each row of another table. If one table has ten rows, and the other table has ten rows, then the product of the join (hence the name, Product Join) will be one hundred rows. With larger tables, the Product Join can result in an enormous number of rows, resulting in substantial system performance degradation. Almost always, a Product Join is the result of an erroneously written query in which the WHERE clause exists, but not the actual join equality condition. Great care should be taken to avoid creating an accidental Product Join.

The following example illustrates a Product Join. The missing equality condition will result in a Product Join:

```
SELECT
E.EMP,
D.DEPT
FROM
EMPLOYEE AS E,
DEPARTMENT as D
WHERE E.EMP > 10;
```

In an SQL statement, the fact that it contains a WHERE clause does not guarantee that it is properly joining the tables. The SQL statement's WHERE clause must join the two tables on a common set of columns. The best way to avoid a Product Join is by making sure that your query is utilizing an equality condition, such as E.DEPT = D.DEPT. If the equality condition is inadvertently left out, a Product Join will occur. In this case, the Product Join is the result of an inequality condition. The optimizer cannot utilize any of the other join strategies because it cannot find the clues it needs in the SQL on how to perform the join. Therefore, a row by row comparison is utilized, as a last resort.

Interestingly, the Teradata optimizer may actually choose to do a Product Join, if it determines that it will actually be the quickest way to perform the join. When a Product Join does occur, the smaller table is copied onto each AMP and the join is performed within Spool space.

Cartesian Product Join

A Cartesian Product Join (also known as a Cartesian Join) is similar to a Product Join. The major difference being that a Product Join is usually the result of an improper WHERE clause, whereas a Cartesian Product Join does not have a WHERE clause. In both cases, the product join occurs due to the lack of a join equality condition.

The following SQL example illustrates a Cartesian Product Join. The missing equality condition will result in a Cartesian Product Join:

```
SELECT
E.EMP,
D.DEPT
FROM
EMPLOYEE AS E,
DEPARTMENT as D;
```

The Cartesian Product Join compares each row in one table with each row of another table. If one table has ten rows, and the other table has ten rows, that means that the product of the join will be one hundred rows. With larger tables, the Cartesian Product Join can result in an enormous number of rows, resulting in substantial system performance degradation. Almost always, a Cartesian Product Join is the result of an erroneously written query in which the join equality condition is missing. Great care should be taken to avoid creating an accidental Cartesian Product Join.

The best way to avoid a Cartesian Product Join is by making sure that your query is utilizing an equality condition, such as E.DEPT = D.DEPT. Keep in mind that if a query joins N tables, than there must be N-1 join conditions. If the equality condition is inadvertently left out, a Cartesian Product Join will occur. In this case, the optimizer in unable to utilize any of the other join strategies because it cannot find the clues it needs in the SQL on how to perform the join. Therefore, a row by row comparison is utilized, as a last resort.

Interestingly, the Teradata optimizer may actually choose to do a Cartesian Product Join if it determines that it will actually be the quickest way to perform the join. When a Cartesian Product Join does occur, the smaller table is copied onto each AMP and the join is performed within Spool space.

Summary

The optimizer will analyze the user's SQL statement and then determine the best plan to successfully complete the query. As discussed throughout this chapter, the optimizer is responsible for determining the best join plan to successfully complete the query.

However, users do have some influence on the join plan. Simple techniques, such as using Primary Indexes (PI) efficiently, and collecting stats on columns that are utilized in the WHERE and ON clauses of your join operations, will provide the optimizer with key pieces of information to ensure that the optimal plan (at that point in time) is used to complete the SQL request.

Chapter 5 - Partitioned Primary Indexes

NPPI
PPI
MPPI
Range_N
Case_N

Teradata has several indexing options that can improve performance on different types of queries and workloads such as secondary indexes, join indexes, and hash indexes. With V2R5.x and later, Teradata has provided a new indexing option known as the Partitioned Primary Index (PPI).

The two types of Primary indexes are partitioned and non-partitioned. Non-Partitioned Primary Index (NPPI) is a traditional primary index by which rows are assigned and stored to AMPs by their row hash value. This provides rapid access to the data when the PI values are specified in a query.

A Partitioned Primary Index (PPI), like NPPI, assigns rows to AMPs by their row hash value. However, the rows are stored based on user-defined data partitions on the AMPs. When PPI partitions are used in queries, they access a portion of a large table, instead of the entire table.

PPI should be utilized to solve specific business requirement(s). Queries that are range-based like comparing month to month, or current month to the previous month of last year on a large detailed table are excellent candidates for PPI tables. Typically, range-based queries with NPPI tables would require a full-table scan, while a PPI table, would only scan a small percentage of the rows in the table.

Primary Index Access (NPPI)

A non-Partitioned Primary Index (NPPI) is a basic primary index by which rows are assigned to AMPs based on their hash value. With an NPPI table on V2R6, the optimizer will store all the rows on Partition (Partition 0) as shown by the illustration below.

NPPI - Order Table

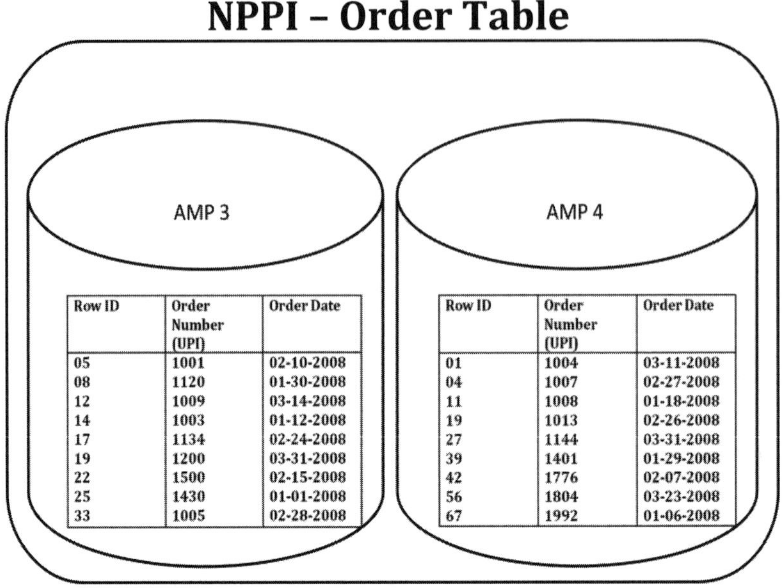

Row ID	Order Number (UPI)	Order Date
05	1001	02-10-2008
08	1120	01-30-2008
12	1009	03-14-2008
14	1003	01-12-2008
17	1134	02-24-2008
19	1200	03-31-2008
22	1500	02-15-2008
25	1430	01-01-2008
33	1005	02-28-2008

Row ID	Order Number (UPI)	Order Date
01	1004	03-11-2008
04	1007	02-27-2008
11	1008	01-18-2008
19	1013	02-26-2008
27	1144	03-31-2008
39	1401	01-29-2008
42	1776	02-07-2008
56	1804	03-23-2008
67	1992	01-06-2008

In this example, the Unique Primary Index (UPI) of the Order Table is Order Number. The Order Number has been hashed and the rows are distributed to the proper AMP(s) based the Row Hash. The AMP will then sort the rows by their Row ID.

Query performance is excellent when a SQL statement (i.e. SELECT) utilizes column(s) of a Primary Index (i.e. SELECT with a WHERE clause that utilizes the equal (=) option). With this type of query, Teradata will retrieve the row(s) on a single AMP as the below SQL statement demonstrates.

```
SELECT Order_Number
FROM Order_Table
WHERE Order_Number = 1005;
```

However, if the SQL statement utilizes a column(s) in the WHERE clause with a range based query (i.e. Between) the end result is a full table scan as the SQL example illustrates below.

```
SELECT Order_Number
FROM Order_Table
WHERE Order_Date
BETWEEN '02-01-2008' AND '02-29-2008';
```

Partitioned Primary Index (PPI) Access

The process of retrieving rows using a PPI table is similar to tables defined with NPPI indexes.

In the example on the next page, the Primary Index is Order_Number and the Partition column is on ORDER_DATE. The Order_Number was hashed to the same AMP as in the NPPI example above.

However, the primary difference is that the data is now sorted based on the Order_Data column. Once the rows are in the partition column, then the Row Hash will store them based on the RowID as illustrated below.

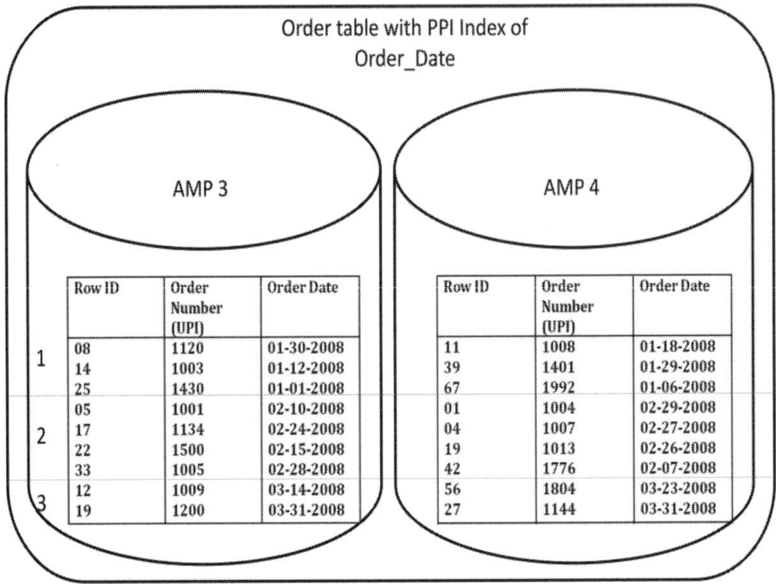

AMP 3

Partition	Row ID	Order Number (UPI)	Order Date
1	08	1120	01-30-2008
	14	1003	01-12-2008
	25	1430	01-01-2008
2	05	1001	02-10-2008
	17	1134	02-24-2008
	22	1500	02-15-2008
	33	1005	02-28-2008
3	12	1009	03-14-2008
	19	1200	03-31-2008

AMP 4

Row ID	Order Number (UPI)	Order Date
11	1008	01-18-2008
39	1401	01-29-2008
67	1992	01-06-2008
01	1004	02-29-2008
04	1007	02-27-2008
19	1013	02-26-2008
42	1776	02-07-2008
56	1804	03-23-2008
27	1144	03-31-2008

If we do the SQL statement below which uses a Between clause and references the partition columns, then the Optimizer will parse the query based on this information.

```
SELECT Order_Number
FROM Order_Table
WHERE Order_Date
BETWEEN '02-01-2008' AND '02-29-2008';
```

The key to using PPI based tables are as follows:

1. RowID values will be stored in different partitions on the AMP. However, once the data is assigned to a Partition, then the RowID values will continue to uniquely identify a row in a PPI table.
2. A RowID will continue to be unique within a partition of a PPI table. However, the same RowID can exist in different partitions depending on the partition columns defined in the table.

Implementing PPI

The PRIMARY INDEX clause of the CREATE TABLE statement followed by a PARTITION BY *partitioning_expression* clause is how you implement PPI based tables. The SQL example below demonstrates how to define a PPI table.

> *Tip* - Keep in mind that if you define your partition on a different column, the Primary Index cannot be a UNIQUE Primary Index.

```
CREATE SET TABLE Order_Table
(Order_Number           Integer
,Customer_number        Integer
, Order_Date            date
, Order_Total           decimal(10,2) )
Primary Index(Order_Number)
Partition by (Customer_Number);
```

The partitioning expression allows users to define characteristics of the table based on business requirements.

In addition, PPI does provide two additional functions for flexibility, which are RANGE_N and CASE_N. These will be discussed later in this chapter.

Partition Elimination and Full Table Scans

The main advantage of a PPI table is the automatic optimization when queries utilize the partitioning column. In the below illustration, data is distributed by the Primary Index (PI), Order Number. However, the data is stored by the Customer Number which was defined by the PPI Create Table statement on the previous page.

> *Tip* - The more partitions there are, the better the potential benefit and performance.

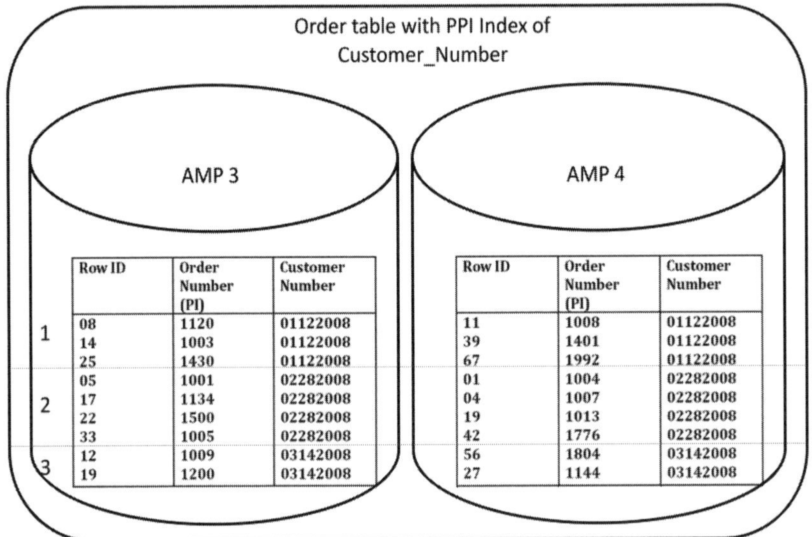

AMP 3:

Partition	Row ID	Order Number (PI)	Customer Number
1	08	1120	01122008
	14	1003	01122008
	25	1430	01122008
2	05	1001	02282008
	17	1134	02282008
	22	1500	02282008
	33	1005	02282008
3	12	1009	03142008
	19	1200	03142008

AMP 4:

Row ID	Order Number (PI)	Customer Number
11	1008	01122008
39	1401	01122008
67	1992	01122008
01	1004	02282008
04	1007	02282008
19	1013	02282008
42	1776	02282008
56	1804	03142008
27	1144	03142008

The query below is requesting orders for a specific customer in the order table. In this example, this query will only read about one-third of the table, instead of the entire table.

```
SELECT *
FROM
Order_Table
WHERE Customer_Number = 02282008;
```

Using Only the Primary Index in a PPI Table

The main disadvantage of using a PPI table occurs when your queries utilize only the PI column as the query below demonstrates.

```
SELECT *
FROM
Order_Table
WHERE Order_Number = 1144;
```

When the PI column is not part of the partitioning column, the Optimizer must look in each partition for that value, instead of directly finding the row based on the PI Row Hash value.

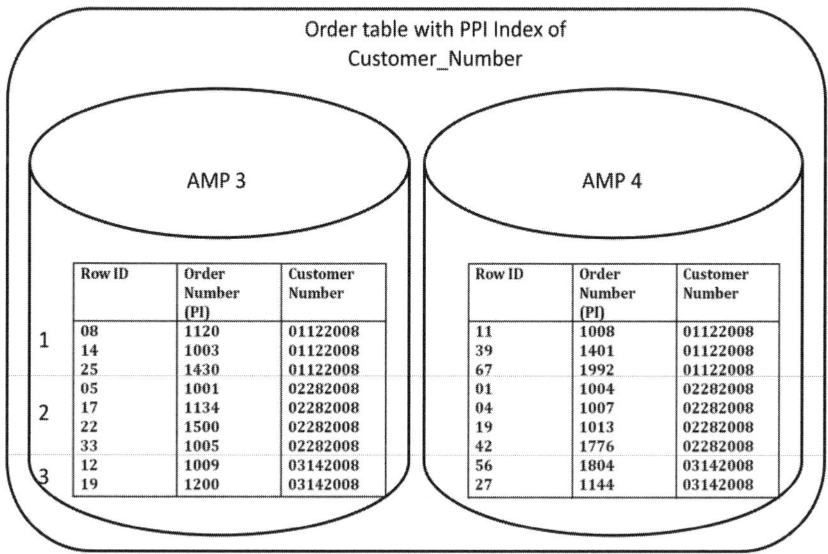

AMP 3

Partition	Row ID	Order Number (PI)	Customer Number
1	08	1120	01122008
	14	1003	01122008
	25	1430	01122008
2	05	1001	02282008
	17	1134	02282008
	22	1500	02282008
	33	1005	02282008
3	12	1009	03142008
	19	1200	03142008

AMP 4

Row ID	Order Number (PI)	Customer Number
11	1008	01122008
39	1401	01122008
67	1992	01122008
01	1004	02282008
04	1007	02282008
19	1013	02282008
42	1776	02282008
56	1804	03142008
27	1144	03142008

With V2R6.x, you can have a range from 1-65535 partitions. The SQL statement below will have to scan every partition.

Keep in mind this query is NOT a full table scan. Instead this is a lookup in all partitions by directly finding the row based on the row hash of the PI column(s).

Using Only the Primary Index on PPI Table Workaround

The worst case scenario with a PPI table is when a query utilizes the PI column when it is not part of the partitioning column. In this situation, we will see an all partition scan on a single AMP in order to find the appropriate PI value. In addition, the number of disk reads could increase to equal the number of partitions on the PPI table. Even though this is a fast operation, a table with thousands of partitions could prove to be a problem for applications that require true PI performance.

Tip – If the Primary Index column is different than the Partition column, then the index must be defined as a non-unique regardless if the column is unique.

One solution is to define a unique secondary index (USI) on the same column(s) as the primary index as shown below.

```
CREATE UNIQUE INDEX (Order_Number)
ON Order_Table;
```

This approach is not as fast as accessing the non-Partitioned Primary Index column. However, a USI is independent of the number of partitions in the table and should provide good performance for applications.

The second option is to ensure that users include the PI and PPI columns in their queries as shown below.

```
SELECT *
FROM
Order_Table
WHERE Customer_Number = 03142008
AND Order_Number = 1144;
```

Partitioning with CASE_N

The CASE_N function provides a simple way to evaluate a list of conditions that will return only rows where the conditions match as this CREATE TABLE demonstrates.

```
CREATE SET TABLE Order_Table
(Order_Number            Integer
,Customer_number         Integer
, Order_Date             date
, Order_Total            decimal(10,2) )
Primary Index(Order_Number)
Partition by  CASE_N
(Order_Total < 10000
 ,Order_Total < 30000
 ,Order_Total < 50000
 ,Order_Total < 75000 , NO CASE , UNKNOWN
);
```

With CASE_N, conditions are evaluated left to right until a condition results in true, unknown, or all conditions have been evaluated. Keep in mind the following when implementing CASE_N functions:

- If the last evaluated condition is true, the CASE_N function returns the position of the condition that evaluates to true. In this case, conditions and options are numbered 1, 2, and 3.
- If the last evaluated condition is unknown, the CASE_N function returns the position of the UNKNOWN or NO CASE OR UNKNOWN option. If neither specified, it returns NULL.
- If all the conditions are false and if there is neither a NO CASE nor a NO CASE OR UNKNOWN option, it will return a NULL.

RANGE_N Partitioning

The RANGE_N function provides a flexible option to define PPI tables based on a specified range of data as shown by the example below.

```
CREATE SET TABLE Order_Table
(Order_Number           Integer
,Customer_number        Integer
, Order_Date            date
, Order_Total           decimal(10,2) )
Primary Index(Order_Number)
Partition by  RANGE_N
(Order_Date between date '2008-01-01' and date '2008-09-30'
EACH INTERVAL '1' MONTH, NO RANGE , UNKNOWN
);
```

With RANGE_N, statements are defined by a start point and an ending point. RANGE_N also allows for multiple ranges to be defined. This is done by specifying start and end points for each of the ranges.

Below are a few easy guidelines to follow when using the RANGE_N function:

- The expression condition evaluated is mapped into one of the specified ranges.
- Ranges are listed in increasing order and must not overlap with each other.
- Results of RANGE_N correspond to a number based on the range. In this case, the number indicates a partition(s).
- RANGE_N columns must be an INTEGER or DATE. (This includes BYTEINT or SMALLINT)

RANGE_N Query Explanation: The Order_Table has been defined with 9 ranges (January - September) and any values that are not in one of the 9 ranges are mapped to either the NO RANGE or UNKNOWN ranges which will be defined as range 10 and 11 respectively.

PPI with Multiple Ranges Defined

The following table is defined with date ranges based on a weekly basis over a 4 year period. If it is determined that access is by week or month, you can re-partition the data accordingly.

```
CREATE SET TABLE Order_Table
(Order_Number              Integer
,Customer_number           Integer
, Order_Date               date
, Order_Total              decimal(10,2) )
Primary Index(Order_Number)
Partition by RANGE_N (Order_date BETWEEN
DATE '2005-01-01' AND DATE '2005-12-31'
EACH INTERVAL '7' DAY,
DATE '2006-01-01' AND DATE '2006-12-31'
EACH INTERVAL '7' DAY,
DATE '2007-01-01' AND DATE '2007-12-31'
EACH INTERVAL '7' DAY,
DATE '2008-01-01' AND DATE '2008-12-31'
EACH INTERVAL '7' DAY, NO RANGE ,
UNKNOWN);
```

However, even though this PARTITION expression is easy to code, it requires more thought up-front along with thoroughly understanding the business requirements.

A simpler partitioning scheme could be used instead by doing the following:

```
PARTITION BY RANGE_N (Order_date
BETWEEN DATE '2005-01-01' AND DATE '2008-12-31'
EACH INTERVAL '7' DAY;
```

Note: Even though the above example is easier in terms of achieving the same ranges, the boundaries for the partitioning scheme defined may not be the same as the first RANGE_N statement.

Implementing Multi-Level Partitioned Primary Indexes

To extend Partitioned Primary Index (PPI) further, Teradata version 12 now supports the capability to create tables or non-compressed join indexes with a Multi-Level Partitioned Primary Index (ML-PPI).

> *Tip* – If PARTITION BY is specified in the table definition, then the table is referred to as a partitioned primary index (PPI) table.

ML-PPI provides the Teradata Optimizer with improved plans by creating sub-partitions on partitions for even further partition elimination, which provides increased granular access to the data and results in better query performance.

When a query is submitted, the optimizer will decide if utilizing the index partition column(s) will provide a benefit to the query plan. If the plan will be improved by using the partitioned index, then the optimizer executes the query accordingly. There are a few considerations when implementing PPI and ML_PPI tables, which are as follows:

- A single-level partitioned primary index, or single-level PPI, is defined when only one partitioning expression is specified.
- A multi-level partitioned primary index, multi-level PPI, is defined when more than one partitioning expression is specified.
- Rows continue to be distributed across the AMPs by way of the Primary Index for both PPI and ML-PPI tables. However, rows are stored and ordered on each AMP by the first partition number, second partition number, etc., and thereafter by hash.
- The use of ML-PPI enables the optimizer to have multiple conditions in the WHERE clause. The result is that the optimizer can do partition elimination to enhance query performance.
- ML-PPI tables that are defined with multi-level partitions can provide flexibility for queries to utilize a combination of the partitions (single or multi). The result is that the optimizer can conduct partition elimination in order to achieve query performance.

With ML-PPI tables, each partitioning level is defined by utilizing separate RANGE_N or CASE_N expressions as the SQL statement below illustrates.

```
CREATE SET TABLE CSQL00.Sales_table_MLPPI
   (
    Product_ID INTEGER,
    Sale_Date DATE FORMAT 'YYYY-MM-DD',
    Daily_Sales DECIMAL(9,2))
PRIMARY INDEX ( Product_ID )
    PARTITION BY (
     RANGE_N(Sale_Date BETWEEN DATE '2007-01-01'
          AND DATE '2007-12-31' EACH INTERVAL '1' DAY),
      RANGE_N(Product_ID BETWEEN 1000 AND 3000
          EACH 1000));
```

The CREATE TABLE example above defines 3 partitions. The first partition range is between 1000 and 1999, the second is between 2000 and 2999, and the third partition only would contain rows that have the value 3000 for the Product_ID,

As depicted in the following diagram, these range-based partitions are combined into a single partition expression, which maps out how the data will be partitioned on each AMP.

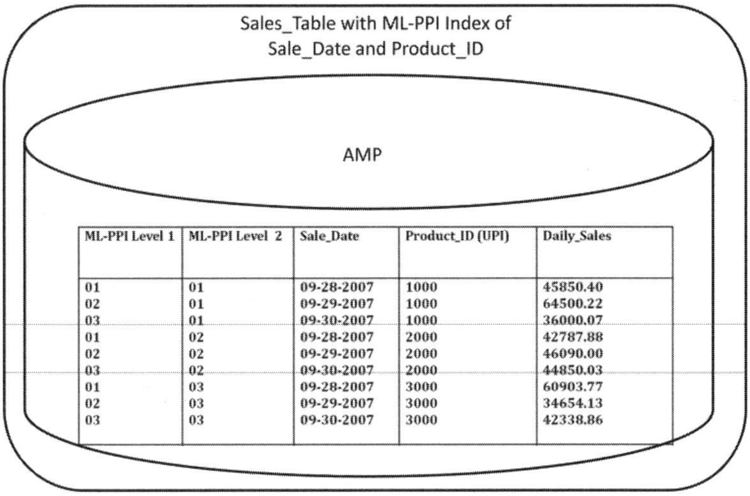

ML-PPI Level 1	ML-PPI Level 2	Sale_Date	Product_ID (UPI)	Daily_Sales
01	01	09-28-2007	1000	45850.40
02	01	09-29-2007	1000	64500.22
03	01	09-30-2007	1000	36000.07
01	02	09-28-2007	2000	42787.88
02	02	09-29-2007	2000	46090.00
03	02	09-30-2007	2000	44850.03
01	03	09-28-2007	3000	60903.77
02	03	09-29-2007	3000	34654.13
03	03	09-30-2007	3000	42338.86

ML-PPI - Examples

Tables defined with ML-PPI will provide access to all partitions in the table, regardless of the number of partition levels that are configured. Partition elimination will occur automatically for queries using partitions, which are specified in the WHERE clause. The result is that the optimizer will take advantage of the partition(s) for better query performance.

Tip – The maximum number of partition levels is 15 and each level must have a minimum of 2 partitions.

The SQL illustration below will eliminate all but one month from the Sales Table, even though the table contains several years of sales. With ML-PPI, this query will access less than 1% of the sales data to complete this query:

```
SELECT Product_ID
        ,Sale_Date
        ,Daily_Sales
FROM   CSQL00.Sales_table_MLPPI
WHERE Sale_Date
  BETWEEN DATE '2007-09-28'
        AND     DATE '2007-09-30'
Order by Sale_Date, Product_ID;
```

In addition, ML-PPI will enable users to utilize other partitions specified in the table other than Sales_Date as referenced above.

The following SQL statement will now eliminate all Product_ID's except those that qualify between 1000 and 1050. This query will access less than 5% of the sales data to complete this query:

```
SELECT Product_ID
        ,Sale_Date
        ,Daily_Sales
FROM   CSQL00.Sales_table_MLPPI
WHERE Product_ID BETWEEN 1000 and
1050
Order bv Product  ID
```

The most optimal query is when you combine both partitions from the ML-PPI table in the WHERE clause as illustrated below.

This query will do partition elimination on both the Sale_Date and Product_ID, which will access less than 1.8% of the sales data assuming even distribution to days and to product ids.

```
SELECT Product_ID
       ,Sale_Date
       ,Daily_Sales
FROM   CSQL00.Sales_table_MLPPI
WHERE Sale_Date
  BETWEEN DATE '2007-09-28'
       AND     DATE '2007-09-30'
And Product_ID =1000
Order by Sale_Date, Product_ID;
```

Rules for ML-PPI

Here are several considerations and restrictions when implementing PPI and ML-PPI tables:

- If you define ML-PPI tables with more than one partitioning expression, you must use either RANGE_N or CASE_N exclusively.
- When you define a ML-PPI table, the number of partitions at each level cannot exceed 65535 which means that maximum number of partitions at a level when there is more than one partitioning expression is 32767. To achieve this maximum, you could only have 2 partitions.
- The maximum number of partition levels is 15.

Tip – Teradata allows up to 15 partitions. However, you could experience diminishing returns if too many sub-partitions are defined. You will need to test your data and your queries to determine where the threshold lies.

Partition Ordering

When defining ML-PPI tables, you also need to consider the order of how the partitions function. The following is a list of important considerations when defining ML-PPI:

- ML-PPI tables, with multiple partitions, are hierarchical in nature.
- The optimizer will still take advantage of partition elimination even if queries access only one-level of a multi-level partition via the WHERE clause.
- You can add partitions to the other levels as long the number of partitions stays the same (that is, you drop as many as you add). For the first level, you can increase the number of partitions using ADD but only up to the point where the product of the number of partitions for each level does not exceed 65535.

Determining the Rows in each Partition

The PARTITION function can be used in SQL Queries. The SQL statement below illustrates how to determine the partition number as well as the number of rows that exist in each partition.

```
SELECT PARTITION as "Partition #"
        ,Count(*) as "Number of Rows"
FROM Order_Table
Group by 1
Order by 1;
```

Note: This query will not show partition numbers for partitions with no rows

The result of the query above will result in the following answer set.

Partition #	Number of Rows
1	1000
2	17655
3	12234
4	32211

Altering PPI Tables to Add or Delete Partitions

The ALTER TABLE statement for PPI tables provides the ability to alter a table in order to perform periodic maintenance on range-based PPI tables.

```
ALTER TABLE order_table
MODIFY PRIMARY INDEX
DROP RANGE BETWEEN DATE '2005-01-01' AND DATE '2005-
12-31' EACH INTERVAL '7' DAY
ADD RANGE BETWEEN DATE '2009-01-01' AND DATE '2009-
12-31'  EACH INTERVAL '7' DAY
 WITH DELETE;
```

This functionality provides a database administrator with the ability to do the following:

- Drop partitions with historical data
- Create partitions for future data
- Re-define both the Primary Index and partitioning expression on empty tables.
- Drop or add ranges at the beginning or end of populated tables.

When working with populated tables, the partitioning expression must be a RANGE_N function. It is recommended that when using this feature, you should drop ranges for the oldest data ranges and add additional ranges for future data that will be loaded. The example below demonstrates this feature.

The ALTER TABLE statement below will drop the partition for date range DATE '2005-01-01' and DATE '2005-12-31'. However, the data will be saved in the Order_2005 table prior to deleting.

```
ALTER TABLE order_table
MODIFY PRIMARY INDEX
DROP RANGE BETWEEN DATE '2005-01-01' AND DATE '2005-12-31' EACH INTERVAL '7' DAY
ADD  RANGE BETWEEN DATE '2009-01-01' AND DATE '2009-12-31' EACH INTERVAL '7' DAY
 WITH INSERT INTO Orders_2005;
```

NO CASE, NO RANGE, or UNKNOWN

The NO CASE or NO RANGE partition is reserved for any value which does not match the defined CASE_N or Range_N expressions. The UNKNOWN partition is used for values where all partitions defined including a NO CASE or RANGE expression are not matched. A typical row that would be assigned to the UNKNOWN partition would be a NULL value as the illustration below demonstrates.

```
Partition by CASE_N
          ( Salary < 10000,
            Salary < 75000,
            Salary < 100000,
            Salary < 1000000,
            NO CASE OR UNKNOWN)
```

Keep in mind that the rows can exist in the NO CASE and UNKNOWN partitions. In addition, rows in these partitions can be accessed for queries. By defining NO CASE and UNKNOWN partitions, you can ensure that all data inserted into this table will be mapped to a partition. If the UNKNOWN and NO CASE partitions are not defined, data values that do not meet the CASE_N criteria will result in errors and will not be inserted into the table.

The example below continues to utilize the NO RANGE and UNKNOWN expressions, but there is no "OR" separating the partition values. In this case, NULLs and all other UNKNOWN rows that do not meet the defined RANGE_N criteria will be stored in the same partition. Therefore, salary being NULL for a row is the only time when that row would be stored in the UNKNOWN partition. All other rows would go to a range partition or to the NO RANGE partition.

```
Partition by RANGE_N
          ( Salary between 10000 and 30000,
            Salary between 30001 and 50000,
            Salary between 50001 and 100000,
            Salary between 100001 and 150000,
            NO RANGE, UNKNOWN)
```

Join Consideration and PPI

In the Join Strategies chapter, we noted that merge joins are options to the Optimizer when we have two tables that have the same primary index (PI or NPPI) and these columns are specified in the ON clause(s) as an equality condition.

This concept is also valid when you do a merge join between two PPI tables that have the same PI and partition columns and these columns, along with the partitioning columns, are included in the ON clause of the join as an equality condition.

In each scenario, the rows on both tables are stored on the same AMPs, therefore, the join operation will proceed with no redistribution of data which makes this an efficient join strategy.

Teradata has also made the optimizer aware of join operations that would occur between PI and PPI tables. This merge join might be slightly slower than a traditional PI merge join. However, if you have a solid partition elimination strategy on the PPI table, then performance should be equal to that of a traditional merge join.

A good strategy (but it is not always available) is to define all of your tables where the partition column and PI's are the same. This would reduce the redistribution and duplication of rows in spool during join operations.

The optimizer has (3) methods when joining PPI to non-PPI (NPPI) tables, and joining two PPI tables that have different partition columns defined. These are as follows:

1. When joining two PPI tables that have different partition columns, the optimizer could choose to spool one or both of the PPI tables in order to convert it to a NPPI table in spool and then complete the merge join.

2. When joining a NPPI with a PPI table, the optimizer may opt to spool the non-PPI table and convert it into a PPI table in spool. This approach would create the new PPI table in spool with the same partition strategy as the base PPI table, which will enable the join to complete on a RowID merge join.

3. When joining NPPI and PPI tables that have the same Primary Index (PI), the optimizer can match the rows based on the PI. From there, the optimizer can determine how many partitions are required from the PPI table to complete the join. In this case, spool will not be utilized to complete the join operation.

With V2R5.1, Teradata provided the ability to perform dynamic partition elimination (DPE). DPE is used when there is an equality condition between the partitioning column of the PPI table and the column in the NPPI table. This works in combination where the number of rows in the NPPI table is relatively small or the number of rows selected from the NPPI tables is relatively small. Of course, utilizing statistics and indexes will make the selection faster and limit the number of rows selected.

This enables the optimizer to match rows based on the condition statement from the NPPI table with matching rows from only the partition required to complete the SQL request. This process of qualifying partitions dynamically is determined by the optimizer and the rows required from the other table to complete the join operation. For example, if there are 100 partitions in the PPI table and only 5 are needed for the join to complete, the other 95 partitions are not used. This provides significant resource savings.

Finally, it is important to make sure statistics are collected on the primary indexes, the partition columns in the PPI table, and the columns in the NPPI table that are the same as the partition column in the PPI table.

PPI Advantages

The greatest advantage of a PPI table is the automatic optimization of queries by the optimizer to do Partition Elimination. For example, queries that only require 6 months of order data from a table that has 7 years of order data can be completed without a full table scan.

> *Tip* – The more partitions defined on the table, the greater the performance (if they are utilized in queries).

There are additional key advantages when you utilize PPI tables correctly in query operations, which are as follows:

- WHERE clauses that are defined on the partitioning column in a query can avoid full table scans. The end result is better performing queries due to partition elimination.
- BETWEEN clauses can now be executed efficiently on tables without secondary indexes defined.
- Partition deletes can be very efficient.

PPI Disadvantage

There are also some disadvantages when using PPI. For example, when joining tables in a query that only accesses the primary index without accessing the partitioning columns, will cause the optimizer do an all-partition scan in order to match rows instead of using only the partitions required to complete the query.

Listed below are additional items you need to consider when utilizing PPI tables. These are as follows:

- PPI rows are 4 bytes longer, hence the tables defined with PPI uses more PERM space
- Secondary index sub-table's row size is also increased by 2 bytes.
- Directly accessing a PI in a query can impede performance if the partition column is not used in the query. This results in an all-partition scan.
- Joins between NPPI and PPI tables with the same primary index can cause performance problems. This is because RowID values will be stored in different partitions on the AMP. This causes additional resources to join each partition on the PPI table to the NPPI table.
- The primary index of a PPI table has to be defined as non-unique if it is not part of the partitioning column of the PPI.

Summary

Partitioned Primary Indexes (PPI) and Multi-Level Partitioned Primary Indexes (ML-PPI) enable users to define tables with partitioned columns to improve query performance via partition elimination while maintaining data distribution by way of the primary index (PI).

A well thought out PPI and ML-PPI plan will transform queries that would typically run as full table scans into high performing queries that only read the data required to complete the request.

As we learned throughout this chapter, there are some trade-offs that need to be understood and carefully considered to ensure that your PPI strategies are maximized to fully utilize this powerful feature.

Chapter 6 - Recursion

Definition
What
When
How

Recursion can best be explained by dissecting a sample recursive statement, which is exactly what this chapter sets out to do. Because of the complexity involved, an entire chapter was devoted to the topic, rather than injecting a blurb under SQL tips. The definition most commonly given to "Recursion" is "refer to Recursion." After the laughter stops, some very beneficial uses for recursive queries may be recognized. From a computer science perspective, the most basic definition of recursion is *"an iterative process whereby a procedure or function calls itself"*.

Recursive SQL is most commonly used for traversing hierarchies. Examples of such hierarchies include a person's ancestry, organizational charts, exploding bill of materials, health group rollups, etc. A common example is to report on all employees under a given managerial level. Another, maybe less obvious use for recursion, is to collapse contiguous dates in a list. We chose the following contiguous date collapsing example to explain how a recursive query works. This can be a very challenging task with any other method.

We are going to pick apart the following recursive query because it is not exactly intuitive. First we set up a table called Attendance, which houses the FROM date and TO date for a person's employment status (i.e. working, off, sick, on vacation, etc.). There is also an indicator for whether they were paid or not.

The recursive query below consists of four sections. The "WITH RECURSIVE" clause defines the temporary recursive table. Within this statement, the anchor or seed statement defines the entry point for the recursive query loop. The recursive section of the loop itself is self-referencing using a case statement to indicate contiguity of the date calculation, and the sequence numbers are referenced to compare to the next row in the group.

The anchor statement and the recursive statement are joined via a union. Note that a "Level" counter is used in order to prevent infinite loops. This level counter is the emergency exit for the recursive statement, and should always be included. The last statement executes the recursive table. Every time the recursive statement executes, it is compared to the prior instance, and the results are appended to the temporary table. It ends when no rows are returned from the recursive statement. This may be due to the level counter being met, or the end of the table has been reached.

Recursive Query Setup - Create Table

```
CT Attendance
(
    From_Dt DATE,
    To_Dt DATE,
    Attendance_Status VARCHAR(10),
    Paid  CHAR(1)
);
```

Insert Test Data

```
INS Attendance ('1990-01-01', '1990-12-31', 'Working', 'Y');
INS Attendance ('1991-01-01', '1991-12-31', 'Time Off', 'Y');
INS Attendance ('1992-01-01', '1992-12-31', 'Working', 'Y');
INS Attendance ('1993-01-01', '1993-12-31', 'Time Off', 'N');
INS Attendance ('1994-01-01', '1994-12-31', 'Time Off', 'N');
INS Attendance ('1995-01-01', '1995-12-31', 'Sabbatical', 'N');
INS Attendance ('1996-01-01', '1996-12-31', 'Time Off', 'N');
INS Attendance ('1997-01-01', '1997-12-31', 'Time Off', 'N');
INS Attendance ('1998-01-01', '1998-12-31', 'Sick', 'Y');
INS Attendance ('1999-01-01', '1999-12-31', 'Working', 'Y');
INS Attendance ('2000-01-01', '2000-12-31', 'Time Off', 'N');
INS Attendance ('2001-01-01', '2001-12-31', 'Working', 'Y');
INS Attendance ('2002-01-01', '2002-12-31', 'Working', 'Y');
INS Attendance ('2003-01-01', '2003-12-31', 'Vacation', 'Y');
INS Attendance ('2004-01-01', '2004-12-31', 'Time Off', 'N');
INS Attendance ('2005-01-01', '2005-12-31', 'Vacation', 'N');
INS Attendance ('2006-01-01', '2006-12-31', 'Sick', 'Y');
INS Attendance ('2007-01-01', '2007-12-31', 'Sick', 'Y');
INS Attendance ('2008-01-01', '2008-12-31', 'Sick', 'N');
```

Recursive Query Example

We developed this rather straightforward example in order to illustrate and focus on the concept of recursion. We want to determine the earliest date and last date this person was paid or not and collapse the dates in between. We are ignoring the status for this example, and returning the contiguous dates that a person is paid or not. Here is the actual Recursive query:

```
WITH RECURSIVE Recursive_Tbl (From_Dt, Earliest_Dt, To_Dt, Paid, Level)
AS
(
-- Seed definition
   SELECT Cur.From_Dt, Cur.From_Dt, Cur.To_Dt, Cur.Paid, 0 AS  Level
   FROM  Attendance  AS Cur
   LEFT JOIN Attendance AS Prev
     ON Prev.To_Dt + 1 = Cur.From_Dt
   WHERE Prev.Paid <> Cur.Paid OR Prev.Paid IS NULL
   UNION ALL
-- Recursive definition
   SELECT Cur.From_Dt,
            CASE WHEN  Prev2.To_Dt + 1 = Cur.From_Dt
            THEN Prev2.Earliest_Dt
            ELSE Cur.From_Dt
            END AS Earliest_Dt,
            Cur.To_Dt, Cur.Paid, Level + 1
   FROM Attendance AS Cur
   INNER JOIN Recursive_Tbl AS Prev2
     ON Prev2.To_Dt + 1 = Cur.From_Dt
   WHERE Prev2.Paid = Cur.Paid
 AND Level < 999
)
-- Executes the Recursive statement
SELECT Earliest_Dt AS Start_Dt, MAX(To_Dt) AS End_dt, Paid
FROM Recursive_Tbl
GROUP BY Earliest_Dt, Paid
ORDER BY Earliest_Dt;
```

Recursive Query Output

Start_Dt	End_dt	Paid
1/1/1990	12/31/1992	Y
1/1/1993	12/31/1997	N
1/1/1998	12/31/1999	Y
1/1/2000	12/31/2000	N
1/1/2001	12/31/2003	Y
1/1/2004	12/31/2005	N
1/1/2006	12/31/2007	Y
1/1/2008	12/31/2008	N

This example has no real gaps in the dates, but the CASE statement above is vital to account for all date gaps. Consider including the status as part of the grouping. To account for multiple people, include a person identifier in the GROUP BY statement.

Now, let's break down this recursive query and discuss its various sections. The following WITH RECURSIVE clause defines a name for the recursive temporary table. Teradata uses the ANSI/ISO SQL standard for the WITH RECURSIVE statement. Within parenthesis, define a list of column aliases to access in the final query.

```
WITH RECURSIVE Recursive_Tbl (From_Dt, Earliest_Dt, To_Dt, Paid, Level)
AS
(
```

The first SELECT statement is commonly referred to as the "Seed" or "Anchor" statement. This statement executes first, giving the recursion a starting point, and the results are stored in the temporary table. All recursive programs need a seed statement, a counter like Level to exit and prevent an infinite loop, and the recursive statement.

```
-- Seed definition
   SELECT Cur.From_Dt, Cur.From_Dt, Cur.To_Dt, Cur.Paid, 0 AS  Level
   FROM  Attendance  AS Cur
   LEFT JOIN Attendance AS Prev
      ON Prev.To_Dt + 1 = Cur.From_Dt
   WHERE Prev.Paid <> Cur.Paid OR Prev.Paid IS NULL
```

This next statement is the recursive select statement that joins back to the original temporary table. Recursive statements are comprised of a UNION ALL of the Seed statement and the Recursive statement. Take note that the CASE statement here is important to account for all date gaps and start the contiguous counting over again if a gap is encountered that is greater than one day.

The Level counter acts as the query terminator, which is defined in the WHERE clause. This is the way out, and all recursive queries should protect against infinite recursion. The Attendance table is joined back to the temporary Recursive_Tbl, and thus the recursion takes place. Every time the statement executes, it is compared to the prior instance, and the results, if there are any, are appended to the temporary table. This statement terminates when no rows are returned from the recursive statement. This may be due to the counter being met, or the table has been exhausted.

```
-- Recursive definition
   SELECT Cur.From_Dt,
              CASE WHEN  Prev2.To_Dt + 1 = Cur.From_Dt
              THEN Prev2.Earliest_Dt
              ELSE Cur.From_Dt
              END AS Earliest_Dt,
              Cur.To_Dt, Cur.Paid, Level + 1
   FROM Attendance AS Cur
   INNER JOIN Recursive_Tbl AS Prev2
      ON Prev2.To_Dt + 1 = Cur.From_Dt
   WHERE Prev2.Paid = Cur.Paid
 AND Level < 999
)
```

The final statement is the Select statement that retrieves the information from the named WITH RECURSIVE temporary table. Make sure to use the correct alias names here that are defined in the first WITH clause. Further aggregations or functions can be performed in this statement or on the output set.

```
-- Executes the Recursive statement
SELECT Earliest_Dt AS Start_Dt, MAX(To_Dt) AS End_dt, Paid
FROM Recursive_Tbl
GROUP BY Earliest_Dt, Paid
ORDER BY Earliest_Dt;
```

Make sure to thoroughly test all results. This can be an extremely powerful tool, but may not solve every problem. Contiguous date processing can become extremely complex, and sometimes columns need to be transposed, edited, etc. Sometimes, it is necessary to compare rows several layers deep and discard some depending on the criteria.

Stored Procedures and cursors offer another possibility, but note that the sequential processing may not be optimal when dealing with large volumes. Incredible performance improvements can be achieved by extracting the data into an ETL tool and programmatically accomplishing the same task in a fraction of the time it takes a stored procedure. Give all alternatives consideration and don't give up.

Recursive View Example

Lastly, let's take a look at a recursive view example. This view can be queried in the same manner that the WITH RECURSIVE temporary table is queried. The view is self-referencing, which makes it recursive.

```
CREATE RECURSIVE VIEW Attendance_Collapse_V (From_Dt, Earliest_Dt, To_Dt, Paid,
Level)
AS
-- Seed definition
   SELECT Cur.From_Dt, Cur.From_Dt, Cur.To_Dt, Cur.Paid, 0 AS Level
   FROM  Attendance  AS Cur
   LEFT JOIN Attendance AS Prev
      ON Prev.To_Dt + 1 = Cur.From_Dt
   WHERE Prev.Paid <> Cur.Paid OR Prev.Paid IS NULL
UNION ALL
-- Recursive definition
   SELECT Cur.From_Dt,
   CASE WHEN  Prev2.To_Dt + 1 = Cur.From_dt  THEN Prev2.Earliest_Dt ELSE
Cur.From_Dt END,
   Cur.To_Dt, Cur.Paid, Level + 1
   FROM Attendance AS Cur
   INNER JOIN Attendance_Collapse_V AS Prev2
      ON Prev2.To_Dt + 1 = Cur.From_Dt
   WHERE Prev2.Paid = Cur.Paid
 AND Level < 999;
```

Querying the Recursive View

Query the view as before with the following:

```
SELECT Earliest_Dt AS Start_Dt, MAX(To_Dt) AS End_dt, Paid
FROM Attendance_Collapse_V
GROUP BY Earliest_Dt, Paid
ORDER BY Earliest_Dt;
```

Capturing Results from Recursive SQL

Finally, how do results get captured from the recursive query and stored in another table? The answer is not necessarily intuitive, but is actually quite simple. The insert clause gets placed prior to the entire WITH RECURSIVE statement as such:

```
INSERT INTO Tbl_Nm
WITH RECURSIVE Recursive_Tbl (From_Dt, Earliest_Dt, To_Dt, Paid, Level);
```

Summary

From a computer science perspective, the most basic definition of recursion is "*an iterative process whereby a procedure or function calls itself*". In Teradata SQL, we use a WITH RECURSIVE statement or a RECURSIVE VIEW definition. Recursion is a somewhat tough concept to grasp and even tougher to summarize, so we set out to explain it by breaking a recursive query example down to its various components or pieces. Recursive SQL is most commonly used for traversing a hierarchy, such as an organizational chart or a person's ancestry.

Chapter 7 - Stored Procedure Coding

Programming
Example
Best Practices
Restrictions

This chapter delves into the specifics of Teradata Stored Procedure (SP) programming and best practices. Throughout this chapter, we will attempt to explain the various components and SQL involved. We will also discuss certain capabilities, error handling, and even some restrictions. External stored procedures are not in the scope of this chapter or this book.

What is a Stored Procedure or SP?

Stored Procedures (SPs) are subroutines or sub-programs coded to perform a set of actions and may (or may not) return some values or out parameters. Teradata is somewhat limited in its ability to return values to the calling program or application. However, result sets are now supported with Teradata Version 12. A typical SP consists of a name, a maximum of 256 input and output parameters, and a body that cannot exceed 6.4 MB. However, there is no limit on the size of the compiled stored procedure or object code.

> *Tip* - Prior to Teradata Version 12.0, you must be logged on as the owner of the SP to compile procedures using dynamic SQL.

Important Note: The person compiling the stored procedure must be logged on as the owner of the procedure because of the dynamic SQL contained within. This has inherent implications that need to be considered prior to coding because the owner of the SP must be a user and not a database. Some of these little restrictions may seem trivial, but they require proper planning and consideration.

"Everything is easier to take apart than to put together."

Let's dissect an actual procedure, and discuss the various pieces individually. The entire code for the following sample SP (CRE_STAGE), mentioned throughout this chapter, can be found in Appendix D. This procedure creates a STAGE table, or any table for that matter, as another table without any Secondary Indices.

It is built on the premise that specifying a primary index in the CREATE TABLE AS statement will leave off any secondary indices. This is the way Teradata currently works, but we can't promise it will always work as such. This is not as efficient, but another way is to drop all secondary indices after the Stage table is built.

Name and Parameter Section

The following piece of code begins the CREATE or REPLACE PROCEDURE statement and states the procedure name.

```
REPLACE PROCEDURE CSQL_PROC.CRE_STAGE (
  IN   STG_DB      VARCHAR(60),      -- Stage DB
  IN   SRC_DB      VARCHAR(60),      -- Source DB
  IN   TAB_NM      VARCHAR(60),      -- Table Nm
  OUT  Orc         INTEGER,          -- Return Code
  OUT  Omsg        VARCHAR(10000)    -- Output Message
)
BEGIN
```

Input and Output parameters are also specified here within parenthesis. It is important to know that Output parameters can be set within the body of the SP, but they cannot be referenced. This program will ask for three input parameters, first being the stage database (STG_DB) or the database where the table will be created. The second and third parameters are the source database and table name that will be copied.

Following the close parenthesis, is a "BEGIN" statement, which begins the body of the stored procedure, and later requires a corresponding END statement to close the body or block. This very well could have been a single SQL or control statement as well instead of the BEGIN ... END block. BEGIN ... END blocks can be nested within the body as well, which is shown later on.

Special Note: This procedure is easily modifiable to pass in another parameter that will indicate whether or not to also include the data.

Comment Section

The next Comment section is optional, but helpful for those who maintain the procedure.

```
/* Program Designer:  Your Name                    Date: July 25, 2009

   Important facts:
-- Until V12, compile as owner of the procedure due to dynamic SQL.
... more comments ...
Purpose: To create STAGE table as a Target table with the same PI and no SIs.  */
```

The programmer should list as many details as possible about the program, especially including the purpose of the procedure and any specific grants that may be needed in order to make it compile. Otherwise, this becomes a guessing game for anyone revisiting the code down the road, including the one who wrote it.

There are two main methods for commenting. Placing two dashes ("--" without quotes) before any text will comment out the rest of any line. Another way to comment out blocks of lines or code is to begin a comment with "/*" and end it with "*/", also without quotes of course. SQL Assistant provides a single button in the Query tool bar to comment out or uncomment single lines or blocks of code. This may seem trivial, but it's very helpful when debugging to quickly comment out large blocks of code at a time.

Variable Declaration Section

All local variables and cursors must be declared prior to referencing them. Try to keep variables consistent across stored procedures. It is a good idea to spend some precious time upfront to come up with conventions and strategies for naming parameters and variables.

For example, you may decide to capitalize INPUT parameters only, or vice versa. Consistency makes programming and maintenance much simpler.

```
-- Variable Declaration Section
DECLARE RetCd       INTEGER  Default 0;
DECLARE Stmt        VARCHAR(10000);
DECLARE CursCnt     INTEGER  Default 0;
DECLARE ColNm       VARCHAR(100)  Default Null;
DECLARE TabTyp      CHAR(1)   Default Null;
DECLARE UniqueTyp   VARCHAR(10)   Default Null;
DECLARE PriorStmt   VARCHAR(10000) Default 'Stmt not set';

-- Cursor Declaration Section
DECLARE  ColCurs  SCROLL CURSOR FOR
SELECT TRIM(ColumnName)||
     CASE WHEN ColumnPosition = MAX(ColumnPosition)
                   OVER (PARTITION BY DatabaseName,TableName)
            THEN ' ' ELSE ',' END AS ColNm,
     CASE WHEN UniqueFlag = 'Y' THEN ' UNIQUE '
             ELSE '' END AS UniqueFlag
FROM  DBC.Indices
WHERE DataBaseName = ''|| :SRC_DB || ''
AND  TableName = ''|| :TAB_NM || ''  AND IndexType='P'
ORDER BY ColumnPosition;
```

In the cursor declaration above, the name of the cursor is ColCurs. This query returns all columns pertaining to the primary index of the source table. Using CASE and MAX...OVER logic simplifies the rest of the stored procedure because no special code is required to treat the last column differently or code for uniqueness. The MAX...OVER identifies the last column and leaves off the comma after the column name.

After declaring all variables and cursors, the nitty-gritty of the code begins. Here we begin a label to make passing control out of the block easier. Multiple labels can be declared and nested, and they may also be used in iteration statements (i.e. LOOP, FOR, WHILE, etc.).

Exit and Exception Handlers

The Exit or Exception Handler is declared to gracefully handle any SQL exceptions. When SQL or fetches within a stored procedure fail for any reason, the program dies or forces complete. The exit handler allows output parameters to be set before ending so that the caller has some idea of what caused the program to abnormally terminate. Without it, the program just ends with a condition code of 0. There is currently no way to report back that a problem has occurred or force a signal.

Note: Teradata Version 13 has user defined exceptions, which will be greatly beneficial.

```
/* Procedure Section */
Lab1: BEGIN
DECLARE EXIT HANDLER FOR SQLEXCEPTION
BEGIN
   SET RetCd=SQLCODE;
   SET Orc=RetCd;
   SET Omsg='SQL ERROR - '|| RetCd ||' Executed following: '|| PriorStmt;
End;
```

Exception handling is a best practice and is crucial to bullet-proofing code, but it is not always necessary depending on the complexity of the task or business need. In the code above code, we set the output parameters to meaningful information, including the true SQL error code. These can then be referenced in the Messages manual.

Input Parameter Validation Section

Partially listed below is the Input Parameter Validation section. Any good programmer initially edits the parameters passed in and displays warnings and exits immediately. Each parameter is evaluated according to the rules that are set, and error codes are returned accordingly. This is obviously a very simple edit, but the rules and code may become much more complex.

Parameter Validation Section

The following code validates a table's existence and captures the type of object that is being refered to as the source table. This program will terminate if the source table is not a table (or TableKind = 'T')

```
/*If  Stage DB name is null, then end with error*/
IF (STG_DB = '') or (STG_DB is Null) or (TRIM(STG_DB) is Null) THEN
    SET Omsg='No Stage Database was entered as 1st Param!';
    SET Orc=31;
    LEAVE Lab1;
END IF;
--Validate Table existence and get Tablekind
BEGIN
    -- Declare Exit handler
    SET PriorStmt='SELECT  TableKind  INTO ... to get Table Kind';
    SELECT  TableKind  INTO :TabTyp
    FROM  DBC.Tables
    WHERE  DatabaseName = ''|| trim(:SRC_DB) || ''
        AND TABLENAME =  ''|| trim(:TAB_NM) || '';
END;

IF TabTyp IS NULL THEN
    SET Omsg= upper(trim(SRC_DB)) ||'.'||upper(trim(TAB_NM))||
          ' Table not found in Database!';
    SET Orc=35;
    LEAVE Lab1;
ELSE
     IF UPPER(TabTyp) <> 'T' THEN
         SET Omsg= 'Table Kind is: '||TabTyp ||
                         ' - Source must be a table and is not!';
         SET Orc=36;
         LEAVE Lab1;
     END IF;
END IF;
```

Continue Handler Section

The following code illustrates the use of a Continue Handler within a nested BEGIN and END block. This code drops the STAGE table prior to recreating it if it exists. Normally, an error would occur indicating that you are trying to drop a table that does not exist. However, this program will continue in this circumstance because of the continue handler. It resides inside a nested BEGIN and END because it would otherwise pass control to the SQL Exception handler declared in the main body or block.

```
BEGIN     -- Drop Table here
    DECLARE CONTINUE HANDLER FOR SQLSTATE '42000'
    BEGIN
      SET RetCd=SQLCODE;
      SET Omsg='SQL ERROR - '|| RetCd ||
                 ' OK to drop if does not exist! '|| Stmt;
    END;
    SET Stmt='DROP TABLE ' ||UPPER(TRIM(STG_DB)) ||'.'
              ||UPPER(TRIM(TAB_NM)) ||';' ;
    CALL DBC.SysExecSQL (:Stmt);
END;
```

Dynamic SQL and Cursor Processing

The rest of the procedure builds and executes the CREATE TABLE AS... statement. This is referred to as dynamic SQL because the SQL is created within the stored procedure and then executed by the stored procedure.

Take note that the CREATE TABLE AS... statement includes the "AND STATISTICS" clause. This is new as of version 6.2 and is quite handy. Statistics or demographic information will be copied over exactly as they exist on the source table as long as the data is copied as well. If "NO DATA" is specified, then the values for the statistical information will be zeroed out.

> *Tip* - As of version 6.2, the CREATE TABLE AS... statement includes the "AND STATISTICS" clause, which will also copy statistical information to the target table.

This is also where the cursor is opened, fetched within a WHILE loop, and eventually closed. A counter (i.e. CursCnt) is used to avoid the possibility of an infinite loop as well as tell the program that the first column name back needs to be treated differently. The first column name initiates the building of the primary index clause, and "UNIQUE" is designated if it is a Unique Primary Index (UPI).

The final CREATE TABLE statement is then initiated by the call to DBC.SysExecSQL. This is a Teradata owned stored procedure, but does illustrate how other personalized stored procedures can be coded and called as well.

Cursor Processing Section

```
-- Start building CREATE TABLE DDL
SET Stmt = 'CREATE TABLE '|| UPPER(TRIM(STG_DB))||'.'||UPPER(TRIM(TAB_NM))||'
AS '||
UPPER(TRIM(SRC_DB))||'.'||UPPER(TRIM(TAB_NM))||'  WITH NO DATA AND
STATISTICS ';

-- Finish building the CREATE with the correct PI
SET PriorStmt='Open ColCurs for first time.';
OPEN ColCurs;
FETCH ColCurs INTO ColNm,UniqueTyp ;
-- CursCnt prevents infinite loop
WHILE (SQLCODE=0) AND (CursCnt < 10000) DO
    IF CursCnt = 0  /*First Column */  THEN
        SET Stmt = Stmt || UniqueTyp ||' PRIMARY INDEX (';
    END IF;
    SET Stmt = Stmt ||trim(ColNm);
    SET CursCnt = CursCnt+1;
    FETCH ColCurs INTO ColNm,UniqueTyp ;
END WHILE;
CLOSE ColCurs;

SET Stmt = Stmt ||');';
SET PriorStmt= Stmt;
CALL DBC.SysExecSQL (:Stmt);

SET Omsg=Stmt;
SET Orc=0;

END Lab1;
END;
```

There are two END statements shown here. The first one ends the label and the second ends the main procedure begin block. Sometimes code is inserted between these two to handle program termination gracefully and perform certain maintenance activities. For example, this is where code may be injected to update a log table, control table, etc.

Compiling

So now the program is finished, how do you compile it? There are several ways, but the simplest way is to log on to SQL Assistant or BTEQ and execute the REPLACE/CREATE PROCEDURE statement directly. Another very useful technique is to write a BTEQ script, which calls the ".COMPILE" command. This way multiple stored procedures can be compiled, or the production implementation of the procedure can be fully automated.

The following script logs on through BTEQ, sets the default database (optional), and then compiles the stored procedure contained in the cre_stage.sql file. This particular piece of code is an extract from a shell script, but doesn't have to be. The rest of the program will resolve the parameters and send log information to the correct destinations.

```
bteq <<EOF
.logon ${DB_ENV}/${LOGIN_NAME},${PW}
.set width 254;
database ${DEFAULT_DB};
.compile file=cre_stage.sql;
.logoff;
.quit;
EOF
```

Debugging

Unfortunately, there is no stored procedure debugger, so it is left up to the programmer to be creative or make no mistakes. Tracing is one technique, which would require inserting information into a debug table throughout the program. You will want to include code to easily turn this on and off, for it will require overhead.

A simpler technique is to set Output parameters in each section with the necessary variable information and force the procedure to terminate with a "Leave" label command or forced exception (i.e. division by zero). Allow time for proper testing.

Stored Procedures Restrictions (Highlights)

Note: Please refer to manuals for a more comprehensive list.

- Prior to version 12, you must be logged in as the procedure owner to compile a stored procedure that uses dynamic SQL.
- Can't use more than 256 parameters.
- The Stored Procedure body size can't exceed 6.4 MB.
- Be careful using ANSI transaction mode and Teradata transaction mode. They can't be compiled and used interchangeably.
- Same parser limits apply if the SQL statements within a stored procedure are very large or complex.
- When calling a stored procedure from a macro, it must be the only statement in the macro like any other DDL statement (same rule).
- EXPLAIN and USING modifiers are not supported.
- Can't use the WITH clause.
- Stored procedures can call other stored procedures, but they can NOT execute macro statements.

Summary

We have just dissected an entire Teradata Stored Procedure down to its various parts. We discussed capabilities, error handling, best practices, and even covered some restrictions. There is no debugger, so it is left up to the programmer to be creative by developing his own debugging or tracing technique.

This chapter was intended to make coding a stored procedure less intimidating. Even though our example is a fairly straight-forward and simple one, many basics and capabilities were covered. Hopefully, the example will be useful, and at the least, act as a stepping stone to greater things. Making DBA life easier starts with automation, so knowing how to properly code stored procedures is a crucial step.

Chapter 8 - Load Strategies

Mini Batch
Trickle Batch
Multiload Direct
Table Refresh

Let's address various load strategies and illustrate reasons for and against each suggestion. This certainly does not address the full gamut of possibilities, but it should be enough to get the brainwaves moving. It is extremely important that DBAs are on the same page when working with Developers and Data Architects in regards to these strategies. The DBAs also need buy-in and understanding from the various Development groups that are using Teradata.

Be sure to conduct learning seminars with each group to discuss chosen load strategies and the importance of each. These strategies should become part of a check list that the DBAs, Developers and Operations personnel adhere to and agree to each time they develop a load process or job. It is of the utmost importance that certain conventions are adopted when loading tables in Teradata. Both Developers and DBAs need to adhere to some standards in order to maintain consistency and protect user and load user access.

DBAs and Developers need to collaborate on the development effort so that the most efficient process is developed with the least impacts to the system and user community. The goal should be to avoid load failures and contention as well.

The first step is to engage the DBA team when it comes to making these decisions, not only to educate them, but also to solicit their opinion and suggestions. DBAs need to be aware of the Development complexities and Developers need to be aware of the database complexities, such as locking, blocking, backups, view layers, etc. Conventions will make decision making and maintenance simpler.

Best Practices and Assumptions

- No one should have access to any tables directly except through at least one layer of base views with Access Locks. Not adhering to this could cause major problems because all tables need to have ACCESS LOCKS before querying them in order to maintain a read-consistent view. User queries could cause load jobs to hang and be blocked.

- Any deviations from the strategies chosen should be reviewed and signed off by the DBA team. They need to account for all load issues, locking anomalies, areas of contention, etc.

- When using FastExport (FEXP) to unload data, there was a time when Teradata suggested that 4 sessions was the optimal setting, and this does seem to work well. Try running some benchmarks to determine what works best for the environment and unload volumes.

Note: The strategies mentioned within this chapter have been simplified to demonstrate the main points. When incorporating security and other business logic, it is quite easy for hierarchies of view databases to become much more complicated than what is depicted as illustrated in this chapter.

Be careful not to set the sessions to hundreds, thousands, or the default of "*". This will default the number of sessions to the number of AMPs on the system, and sessions could be easily used up altogether. There seems to be a law of diminishing returns as sessions are added, and at a certain point loads will actually slow down. Depending on the amount of data, it could take longer to log on and off all the sessions than to load the data. Test and find some numbers that work best and stick with them.

Strategy 1 - Using an ETL Tool

If using an ETL tool, be careful not to use the ODBC interface to load anything much larger than a reference table. Try limiting the use of these options to volumes less than a few thousand rows or even to a few hundred rows. Establish your own limit of 10,000 rows or so, but please note the ramifications to the query logs.

Why limit the use of this strategy? This approach seems to cause DBQL to log multiple entries for every row that is loaded into the target table (acting like MS ACCESS). Depending on current DBQL settings, there could be other DBQL tables affected as well, like the Object table, Step table, and SQL table. It basically logs a separate insert statement for every individual row. This totally skews DBQL information and reporting and has the potential to waste a tremendous amount of space.

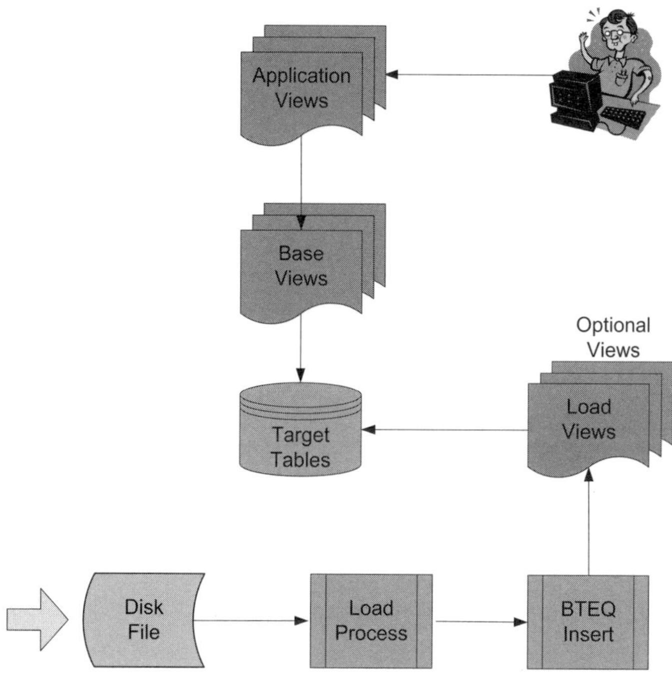

When to Use

- Use this for small reference tables or small increments of data.
- Used by ETL tool.

Cons

- Increased DBQL logging mentioned above.

Strategy 2 - Trickle Feed Batch with BTEQ

This refers to appending small increments of data on to a preexisting table. This technique is used to append a few rows to a few hundred rows in a more frequent time frame. This is not to say that thousands of rows or more can't be loaded, but its feasibility needs to be tested first. There are factors such as table sizes, Join Indices, and secondary indices that need to be considered and tested. Don't target this process for hundreds of thousands to million row increments.

This process entails using BTEQ to do a direct insert into the target table from a load-ready file. There is no need to STAGE the data first. This will NOT require a dual table or dual database architecture, so only a single table needs to be targeted.

When to use

- When loading a very small number of rows from a data file.
- Writing your own scripts (easy) – not using tool.

Side Note: If fortunate enough, an alternative strategy is to use TPUMP for appending small incremental numbers or trickling in data.

Strategy 3 - MultiLoad Direct Appends

This refers to adding or appending larger amounts of data to preexisting tables using MultiLoad directly to target tables without staging. Although there are problems posed with this strategy, the process is relatively straightforward. The TPT Update operator can also be used in place of MultiLoad, but we will refer to MultiLoad for the remainder of this section. These two products use the same code base.

As illustrated below, this process uses MultiLoad to load the tables directly utilizing the LOAD views. Load views are optional; however, they do give the added benefit of being able to load multiple locations simply by changing where the load views point, and avoiding the need to alter code or job parameters.

Multiload Direct

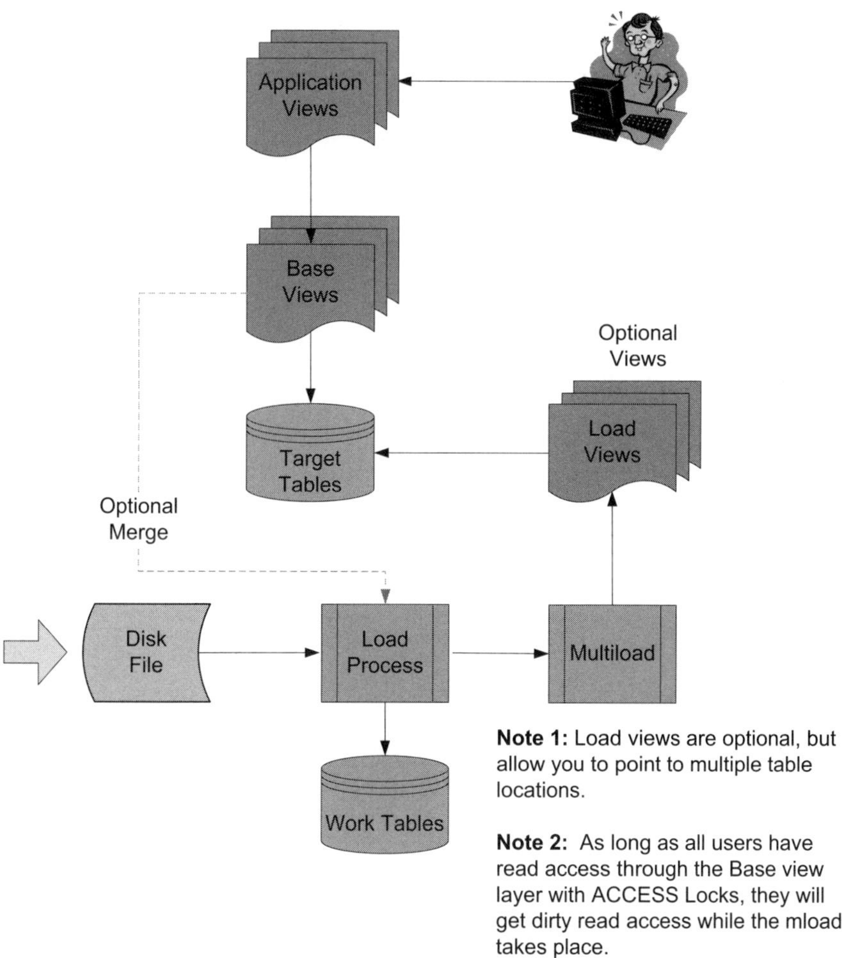

Note 1: Load views are optional, but allow you to point to multiple table locations.

Note 2: As long as all users have read access through the Base view layer with ACCESS Locks, they will get dirty read access while the mload takes place.

When to use

- Large or small volumes.
- Loading multiple tables simultaneously.
- No Unique Secondary Indexes exist on the target tables.
- Data append – not full refresh of data.
- Load is completely without issues or failures.
- NOT performing RELEASE MLOADs on the target table during the load.

Cons

- Failures at certain points in the load will cause the table to remain in a MultiLoad Load state and unusable. Release MLOAD may or may not work at this stage. If the release does not work, then the table may need to be restored.

- It is a common practice for developers to perform RELEASE MLOAD commands before every Multiload job for restartability. We do not advocate this process because it forces an exclusive lock on the target table, and causes possible contention between load processes and user queries. Access Read locks will still wait and queue behind Exclusive locks, and vice versa. The load job will now wait if queries are running against the target table because it needs to get and exclusive lock.

- MultiLoad does not execute on tables with Unique Secondary indices, referential foreign constraints, or Join Indices. Therefore, a workaround is needed anyway, like dropping and recreating the indices. This too requires exclusive access, and other overhead.

Strategy 4 - Mini Batch Data Appends

This refers to adding or appending large or small amounts of data to preexisting tables using STAGE tables. Although there are problems posed with this process as well, the resolution is fairly straightforward and simple.

The mini batch process will first load or stage the data into an empty table at high speeds using TPT, MultiLoad or FastLoad, and then insert...select the data into the target table. Since all tables will be accessed by users through views with ACCESS LOCKS, anyone reading the tables will still get a READ ACCESS LOCK on the table.

If users are already accessing the table, then they will get a "Dirty Read". This approach will also NOT require a dual table or dual database architecture, so the target is only a single table.

The following lists some different ways to stage tables in order of preference. This shows the preferred method for creating staging tables is to dynamically create them without indexes.

- One way is to dynamically perform a CREATE TABLE AS ... WITH NO DATA at the time of the load. This is excellent for restartability because the stage table can simply be dropped and recreated at the beginning of every load. It also avoids having to maintain consistency between the stage table and the existing target table. This would be required if a permanent stage table was chosen instead. Leaving the stage table accessible between loads is also great for diagnosing problems.

  Challenge: The down side of this method is that indexes really need to be dropped if there are any on the target table. This could cause some programming issues, but we address how to resolve this issue easily.

  We developed a stored procedure and provided it for you in Appendix D. This stored procedure identifies the primary index of the target table and then creates the stage table with an identical primary index. Specifying the primary index in the CREATE TABLE ... AS statement causes the automatic removal of any secondary indexes. This is the fastest method, but an alternative is to create the stage table as the target table, and then systematically drop every secondary index by traversing a cursor.

> *Tip* - The preferred method for creating staging tables is to dynamically create them without indexes.

- Another method is to create and maintain a permanent STAGE table, and delete all records prior to performing a FastLoad, TPT Load, or MultiLoad on it. This is still very good for restart capability and diagnosing problems if something goes wrong. The down side is that this stage table must be maintained and kept in sync with the target table. The other problem is that the load user may need drop and create access if a FastLoad fails and the tool being used is unable to clean up the failed FastLoad.

- A less likely method is to use Global Temporary tables. However, if something goes awry, there is nothing to diagnose the problem with.

- This staging technique can also be used to perform a full table refresh, but this is not strongly advocated. If this alternative is chosen for such a requirement, make sure the target table is not large (few hundred thousand rows or less) and inserted in a second or two. Make sure to fully load a Stage table first, validate it, and then quickly perform a delete all and insert from the stage table. If a user happens to query the table during this process, it may actually see an empty table at one point, but the timing needs to be exact. By staging and validating everything prior, downtime is diminished for the user.

Mini Batch

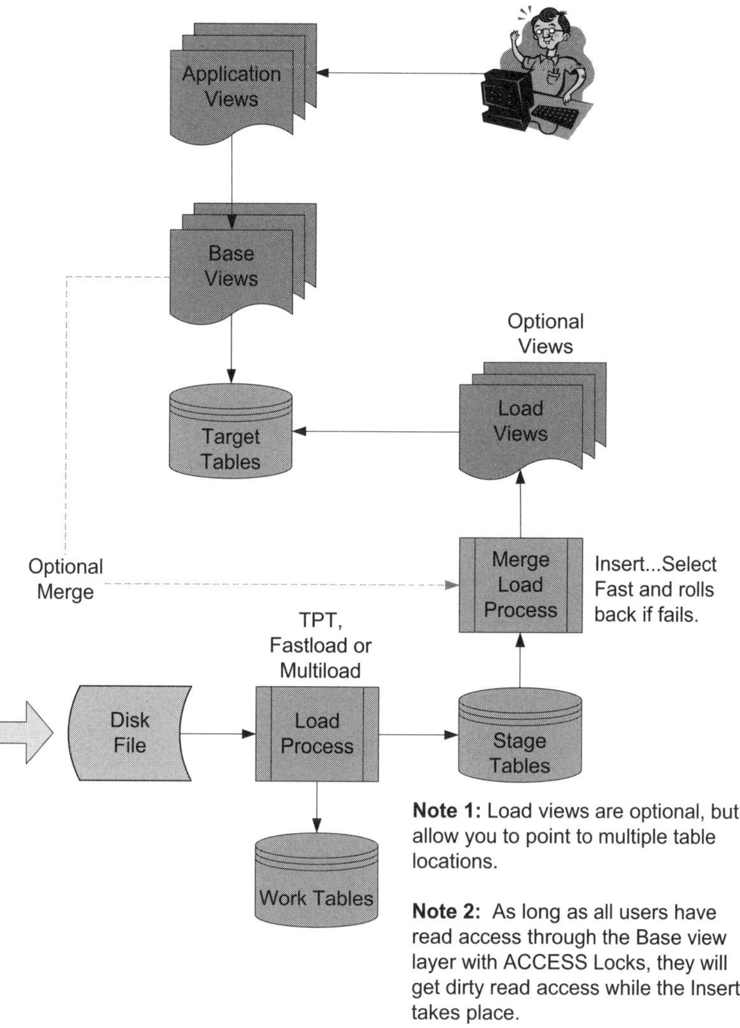

Note 1: Load views are optional, but allow you to point to multiple table locations.

Note 2: As long as all users have read access through the Base view layer with ACCESS Locks, they will get dirty read access while the Insert takes place.

When to use

- When loading small or large volumes.
- Used for incremental or full table loads.
- Avoids user contention.
- Even with the extra insert, this technique is fast if using TPT or FastLoad for the initial stage load.
- If the desire is a truly restartable process.
- To overcome many of the deficiencies of the direct MultiLoad strategy. When MultiLoad Direct fails, the target table is left in an unusable state. This can't be allowed, and can leave the users without access for an indeterminate amount of time. With the Mini Batch, if the insert fails, it just rolls back and the table is still accessible.
- This will also work for Unique Secondary Indices, Join Indexes, etc. on the target table. There is no need to drop and recreate indexes on the target table.

Cons

- Rollbacks may be costly, so the load process must be careful to avoid loading problematic rows to the target table. Later Teradata Releases (12.0) will allow the creation of error handling tables, so problems like duplicates and other errors would go to these error tables instead of rolling back.
- Dirty reads imply possible inconsistent views of the data as the data gets loaded, updated, deleted, etc. The only way to avoid this is to have daily outages and revoke access at certain points or allow the tables to be locked. This will cause contention in the load process.

Strategy 5 - Full Table Refreshes

This refers to fully deleting and replacing all data on the table. We strongly suggest that limiting the use of this strategy as much as possible. Try adopting a new ETL strategy. For example, any point-in-time changes may need to be performed incrementally.

This strategy requires a dual table or dual database architecture in order to fully avoid all blocking scenarios. We have chosen a dual database design (illustrated below) to accommodate the developers' desires to always load the same table name, and because the view switching technique can be easily handled via a stored procedure.

The following design will allow users to continue their normal access to tables during full loads, index builds, and statistics collection. No one waits on anyone and there are no blocking issues on either end. When the first table is fully loaded and ready, simply switch the base view and the load view.

This can be accomplished in a similar fashion with a dual table design within the same database. However, this poses its own challenges to overcome. Here are some thoughts to consider.

- Do you switch the views or rename the tables each time and how do you maintain the active table?
- It's really important to realize that renaming two tables will require an exclusive lock on both tables at some point in time.
- How do you perform backups? Backing up the database may require backing up twice the space needed each time.
- Then there are flexibility issues for the ETL developers. There are pros and cons to both approaches.

Special Suggestions

- FastLoad and TPT's Load operator do not allow loading into tables via views. Although this is limiting, it is better to dynamically create stage tables, use FastLoad or TPT to load the data in, and then insert-select into the target via a view.

- Views are helpful because they allow control over what table is targeted for the load, without changing the ETL code or parameters each time. TPT's Update operator uses the same code base as MLOAD and does allow loading through views.

- If any Unique Secondary Indices (USI), Foreign Key references, Hash Indexes, or Join Indexes exist on the target table, then they must get dropped before using MultiLoad to load the tables directly. Afterward, the indices can be recreated after the load, which may not be a simple process to code or maintain. This process can also be very time-consuming and resource intensive.

- A better alternative first loads either a permanent, or better yet, dynamically creates a staging table and then loads the target table with an insert-select. The dynamic table gets created using a stored procedure and eliminates any secondary indexes. This part of the process is depicted as optional in the illustration below.

- When MultiLoad fails, the target table is typically left in an unusable state. This can leave the users without access for an indeterminate amount of time. Therefore, we suggest not loading directly to the target table via MultiLoad. Try loading the data into a stage database first via FastLoad or TPT. Then the rows can be validated prior to inserting them into the target table.

Full Table Refresh

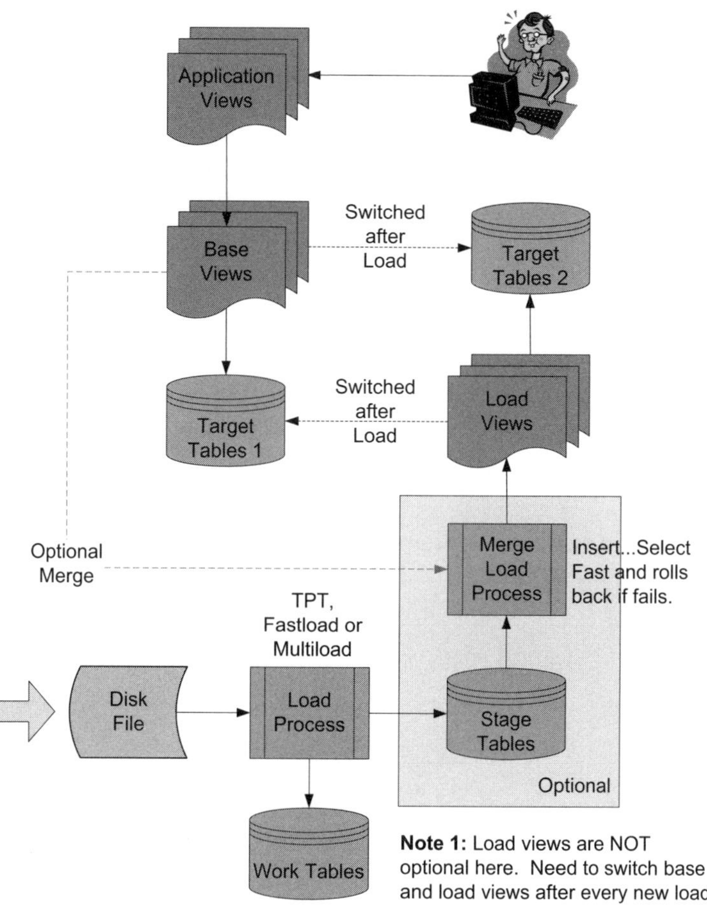

Note 2: Staging the data is optional here. It still may be faster to Fastload into the stage area and copy the data over.

When to use

- Use this technique when fully replacing data in a table, and when wanting to maintain no downtime for the user community. Full table refreshes pose a particular problem because it is hard to simultaneously maintain both a read-consistent view of the data and avoid downtime, especially on large tables.
- Make every effort to design the process so that contention is eliminated between both users and load processes. They are not mutually exclusive, and the design needs to accommodate both, ensuring that neither can block the other.
- Only use when absolutely necessary, and when the source of the data will not support the incremental load capability in any other way.

Cons

- There are either two target databases or two target tables to maintain, collect stats on, etc.
- The method used to switch base views after every table load needs to be efficient, flawless and easy.

Summary

This chapter discussed various techniques or possibilities for loading data into Teradata as well as their benefits and short-comings. There are many more possibilities, but the point is to document the benefits and costs of each so you can use the correct strategy for a given situation. It is important to establish conventions and standards for loading data, and then make sure these standards are enforced.

It is up to the DBAs to work with the Developers and Data Architects to help them understand the strategies and when to use them. Be sure to come up with ideas that will protect both users and load processes by eliminating possible contention between them. The goal of the load process should be to avoid load failures and be as efficient as possible. Hopefully, this chapter will help ignite ideas for the reader.

Chapter 9 - Statistics

Collection
What
When
How

The Teradata optimizer depends on statistics in order to formulate the least costly join plans and access paths to the data. Without statistics, the optimizer relies on random AMP samples that only provide limited demographic information. Random AMP samples are not comparable to full stats, and were designed to just provide a quick table row count estimate

The optimizer already knows about the system configuration, such as the disk array configuration, memory, number of nodes and CPUs. In order to make accurate execution plans and cost estimates, the optimizer also needs to know about certain demographic information such as the number of rows in the table, number of rows per block, number of rows per value, index columns, and column values. Statistics provide the optimizer with this vital information.

While it is impressive to know how Teradata internally stores statistics or column demographics in histograms and how the optimizer makes use of this demographic information, we chose to focus on other crucial questions such as:

Should we collect on small tables?
Should we collect on indexes over columns?
How do we identify columns to collect on?
How often should we collect?
Can I collect on Join Indices and Temporary tables?
How do I determine what columns have Statistics on tables?
What are some other important limitations?

Here are some important points to be aware of:

- Collecting statistics can be very resource intensive, especially on larger tables, so it is important to plan when and on what to collect.

- The collection process inherently places access locks on the target tables, so that is one thing less to worry about.

- Be wary of relying on sampled statistics or random amp samples due to their current reliability. Sample stats in version 12 and V2R6 releases can be reliably used for unique columns or near-unique columns only. Teradata 13 uses a new, improved algorithm for sampled statistics, which may make them somewhat more useful than in previous releases.

- There is a 16 byte limit on the length of the combined values that can be stored in the statistic histogram intervals, and statistics are stored in the order that they appear in the DDL. This makes the order important for longer fields.

- Also, take note that VARCHAR and CHAR are case-sensitive in histograms, so consider standardizing on case if the statistics are important.

- When creating tables, keep longer (i.e. VARCHAR(30)) fields toward the end of a column list in the CREATE TABLE statement.

Tip – When creating tables, keep longer (i.e. VARCHAR(30)) fields toward the end of a column list in the CREATE TABLE statement.

With regard to the last bullet, multicolumn stats are stored in the data dictionary in the order that they appear in the create table statement DDL. Since only 16 bytes will ever get stored, larger data types upfront will cause truncation of multicolumn stats and lost information for the optimizer.

This is best illustrated by example. Let's take a scenario where multicolumn statistics are required on three columns (Course_name VARCHAR(30), Credits BYTEINT, and Seats BYTEINT). If they appear in this order in the DDL, then Credits and Seats will have no presence in the histogram for any Course_names greater than 16 characters, and the whole "combination" is negated.

Consider the following as well, any Course_names where the first 16 characters are the same as others will be considered and counted the same. For example, "Introduction to Dinosaurs" will be considered the same as "Introduction to Diving" because the first 16 characters are identical.

COLLECT STATISTICS is the command used at the table, column, or index level to capture statistical or demographic information about column values, whether it's a single column or multiple columns. This information is stored in the data dictionary and used by the optimizer.

Single Column Example

```
COLLECT STATISTICS ON Tbl_Nm COLUMN Col_Nm1;
```

Multicolumn Example

```
COLLECT STATISTICS ON Tbl_Nm COLUMN (Col_Nm1,
Col_Nm2);
```

Index Example

```
COLLECT STATISTICS ON Tbl_Nm INDEX Index_Nm;
```

Partition Column Example

```
COLLECT STATISTICS ON Tbl_Nm COLUMN PARTITION;
```

Global Temporary Table Example

```
COLLECT STATISTICS ON TEMPORARY Temp_Tbl_Nm
COLUMN (Col_Nm);
```

Sampled Statistics Example

```
COLLECT STATISTICS USING SAMPLE ON Tbl_Nm
COLUMN (Col_Nm1, Col_Nm2);
```

Should we collect on small tables?

The optimizer uses statistics (in the form of histograms) when building an execution plan for a query. Teradata only has random AMP samples and fixed formulas that are used when no statistics are available to rely on to make these assumptions. This brings us to the first important rule. Collecting statistics on small and skewed tables is every bit as important (if not more so) as collecting on large tables.

> *Tip* - Collecting statistics on small and skewed tables is every bit as important (if not more so) as collecting on large tables.

For example, consider a 90-AMP system and a Gender table that has 3 values (Male, Female, and Unknown). Without statistics, the optimizer will conduct a random AMP sample, and have a 3-in-90 or 1/30th chance at best of obtaining accurate information.

The default for randomly selecting data is by a single AMP, which can be modified by working with Teradata to change an internal field called RandomAMPSampling in the DBSControl record. Random AMP Sampled statistics are more accurate for larger, well distributed tables, so don't rely on them for smaller skewed tables.

SAMPLE statistics can be collected with the USING SAMPLE syntax, but Teradata will be the first to admit that the quality of sampled statistics is no substitute for the real thing. The quality of USING SAMPLE statistics is unreliable for all but unique or near-unique data. These statistics are captured from taking the first 2% (by default) of the table on each AMP.

Random AMP samples are just an option to having no statistics collected at all, and will result in the optimizer making more conservative choices than if it were using full statistics. USING SAMPLE statistics does have a slightly better algorithm than random AMP samples for making estimates on skewed tables. Random amp sampling seems to be much more accurate for larger more evenly distributed tables.

A common problem DBAs and Developers run into when designing ETL processes stems from having to grant Index to the load user on every table in order to collect statistics on it. This requires the DBA to be diligent and always remember to continually grant this privilege any time the table is dropped and recreated.

An easy alternative is to grant DROP TABLE to the user on the database, but that is a dangerous practice for obvious reasons. The other problem with both of these practices is that statistics need to be recollected on the correct columns every time a table is recreated so that any ETL processes don't fail when they collect at the table level.

A somewhat complicated but more desirable alternative is to create an intelligent stored procedure whose owner has the DROP TABLE privilege at the database level for all databases that contain tables. This stored procedure will be discussed later, but can be designed not to fail through control tables and column and index defaults.

Special Note: In Teradata 13, there is a new statistics collection privilege. However, this does not negate the entire purpose of the intelligent stored procedure.

Should we collect on indexes over columns?

> *Tip* - Always collect on the "PARTITION" column of PPI tables so that the optimizer makes accurate cost decisions. Collecting on the partition performs quickly with minimal impact. Partition statistics can't be gathered on global temporary, volatile, or Join Indexes.

When given the option, it is generally faster to collect on the index rather than the individual column(s). There was a time when statistics would be lost or dropped if an index was dropped, which would dissuade someone from following this rule. However, current versions of Teradata keep the statistics on the columns that comprise the index even if the index is dropped. It is good practice to always test these suggestions on the current version of Teradata.

For Partitioned Primary Index (PPI) tables, collecting stats on the column PARTITION can provide the optimizer an accurate cost to the operation by giving precise information as to how many partitions are actually populated.

In older versions of Teradata, it was not a good practice to over allocate partitions because the optimizer would make decisions based the number of partitions in the table, which may be grossly exaggerated. For example, in order to minimize maintenance activities on a table, DBAs would allocate a monthly range partition on a date several years into the future. With this approach, the optimizer would make poor decisions based on the assumption that there were hundreds of partitions, even though only a dozen or so were actually populated.

Given the above example, the best practice at this time and for older versions of Teradata was to keep the number of partitions as accurate as possible in order to avoid miscalculations by the optimizer. This was difficult to manage and required some significant programming to automate.

RANGE_N range partitions can be added or dropped on populated tables. Always collect on the "PARTITION" column of partitioned tables so that the optimizer makes accurate cost decisions. Collecting on the PARTITION performs quickly with minimal impact. Prior to Teradata 13, PARTITION statistics can't be gathered on global temporary, volatile, or Join Indexes. With Teradata 13, you can collect PARTITION statistics on volatile tables and join indexes, but not global temporary tables.

How do we identify columns to collect on?

There are differing opinions on how to determine which columns to collect on, but a good starting point is to collect on primary index and index columns at a minimum.

From there, decisions to collect statistics on additional columns are based on frequency of use and resource windows. However, we suggest collecting statistics on as many columns as possible for very small tables because they don't require heavy resource usage. We recommend that you avoid description and comment type fields, but since small reference tables require such little resources to collect, it would not hurt much to collect on these fields as well.

Once tables reach a certain size (different for all systems) where resources are taxed and collection times are no longer negligible, then it is important to be more particular during the decision making process. At this point, concentrate on columns that are commonly used in WHERE, ON, AND, and IN clauses of views and common user SQL.

The Teradata Statistic Wizard helps identify statistic candidates on a given workload or on the SQL statement by itself. An alternative is to use the following command and perform an Explain after.

Setting Diagnostic HelpStats

```
diagnostic helpstats on for session;
Explain Select ...;
```

If they exist, statistic recommendations will be found at the bottom of the Explain Plan. The Explain Plan may be overly aggressive in its recommendations for combinations of single and multicolumn statistics. From there, the user can apply these suggestions as needed to optimize query performance.

It will even suggest multicolumn combinations on Join Indexes that can't be applied. For example, it is not possible to collect multicolumn statistics on a Join Index, unless a secondary index is already defined on those columns. Collecting on every suggestion is not necessary, but it's a good idea to start with the single column suggestions.

How often should we collect?

A common rule of thumb is to collect statistics on the following:

- Immediately after loading a table for the first time
- When upgrading to a new Teradata release
- Every time the data demographics change by 10% or so.

There are many different opinions on whether a 10% change in the number of rows is needed or the demographics of the columns need to change by that much. Then there is the question as to when to collect on partition tables. Do you collect when the number of rows in the table changes by 10% or when the partitions change by 10%? As one can imagine, this can get quite complicated, so certain lines may need to be drawn.

Although it's probably more accurate to identify when the cardinality of the values in the column change by 10%, we chose a fairly simple (KISS method) and more conservative alternative. First, we refresh or recollect the statistics once per week in full on all tables during a period of low activity (i.e. Sundays). Then we recollect during the week only if the table size changes by 8% in either direction.

The use of a stored procedure here for calculating the 8% by comparing it to the table size at the last full table collection provides a good method on when we should collect statistics. We use the table size because we can quickly get this information from the data dictionary and don't have to perform a full table scan to get row counts or cardinality change counts.

It is important to know that stale or old statistics are actually worse than no statistics. It's a common practice to collect stats when tables are empty or newly created in order to identify which columns to collect on going forward. Make sure to recollect at the table or column level immediately after the table is initially loaded. This will absolutely destroy performance if this minor detail is overlooked.

Finally, we recommend collecting statistics on PARTITION columns when partitions change by 10% or new partitions become populated. This process seems to be fairly efficient and fast anyway.

Can I collect on Join Indices and Temporary tables?

Statistics should be collected on all Join Indices and Hash Indices, just as would be done on base tables, but there are limitations. For instance, multicolumn statistics cannot be collected on Join Indices unless there is a secondary index predefined on those columns. As of version 6.2, SAMPLED statistics cannot be collected on Hash Indices, Join Indices, or Global Temporary tables.

Only the explain plan will disclose whether the query uses the Join Index or not. We've seen it work both ways, where no statistics reside on the Join Index and the parser chooses to use the Join Index anyway. Then when statistics get collected, the explain plan no longer shows the Join Index being used. However, this is not typically the case, and the statistics are usually necessary for the optimizer to choose the Join Index.

Collection is possible on Global Temporary tables, but collecting on volatile tables is not available at this time. Collecting on temporary tables requires the key word "TEMPORARY" before the table name as depicted below.

Global Temporary Table Example

```
COLLECT STATISTICS ON TEMPORARY Temp_tbl_nm;
```

The syntax above assumes that statistics are already collected at the column or index level for this temporary table. Collecting statistics on Global Temporary tables requires that you follow the following process:

- CREATE the Global Temporary table.
- COLLECT STATISTICS on the Indexes and Columns.
- INSERT data into the Global Temporary table.
- Recollect statistics using the key word TEMPORARY.

How do I determine what columns have Statistics on tables?

The SQL command used to determine what statistics exist on a table is the HELP STATS or HELP TEMPORARY STATISTICS if it's a temporary table. This command will work with STAT, STATS, or the word STATISTICS.

Help Statistics Example

```
HELP STATISTICS Tbl_Nm [COLUMN Col_Nm];
```

Help Statistics on Temporary Table Example

```
HELP TEMPORARY STATS Temp_Tbl_Nm;
```

The above commands return a line of output for each statistic that has been explicitly collected along with the Date, Time, and number of Unique Values for each statistic. Histograms are kept in the data dictionary in DBC.TVFields or in DBC.TVIndexes.

This information can also be derived from the MultiColumnStats and ColumnStats views in DBC or by joining several tables with DBC.TVFields. However, deriving the statistical information from the ColumnStatistics or FieldStatistics columns can be quite arduous. Various websites provide this information, but it's nice to know that Teradata plans to make this information more easily accessible via the catalog in upcoming versions.

What are some other important limitations?

- Because it is not possible to collect statistics on a volatile table, statistics can't be copied for a volatile table either.

- PARTITION statistics are not copied from the source table to the target table if an explicit index definition is specified for the target table.

- PARTITION statistics are not allowed on global temporary tables, volatile tables, or Join Indexes. In Teradata 13, statistics can be collected on volatile tables and Join Indexes

- There is still no way to collect statistics on a particular partition or new partition. However, in Teradata 12, they are extrapolating statistics which should help.

- As of version 6.2, SAMPLED statistics can't be collected on Hash Indices, Join Indices, or Global Temporary tables. In Teradata 13, sampled statistics work with join indexes.

- The system does not store both defined and SAMPLED statistics for the same set of columns or indices. An implicit call to COLLECT STATISTICS will use the most recent mode collected.

- Sampling statistics on the PARTITION column will result in a 100% sampling anyway, and sampling on columns that are part of a PPI expression are not allowed.

- Statistics should be collected on multi-table Join Indices because the statistics collected on the base tables are not exchangeable. However, the optimizer often carries forward the base table statistics to single table Join Indices.

Summary

Statistics provide the Teradata optimizer with vital demographic information on tables and columns in order to make accurate execution plans and cost estimates. If statistics are missing, then Teradata relies on random AMP sampling, which is unable to detect skew and can lead the optimizer to poor decisions. Therefore, devise a method like the one mentioned earlier to keep the statistics fresh and up to date.

When given the option, it is generally faster to collect on indexes rather than the individual column(s). There was a time when statistics would be lost or removed if an index was dropped, but now these statistics remain. Lastly, collect on the "PARTITION" column of PPI tables so that the optimizer estimates partition-related decisions correctly.

Chapter 10 - Compression

Performance
Space Reduction
Financial Savings

Compression allows multiple values to be compressed on a fixed-width column up to 255 distinct values plus NULL. By deploying this technique, you have the ability to buy back storage capacity, improve response time, and possibly reduce disk I/O and CPU utilization. While improved storage capacity can be immediately and easily recognized, it is more difficult to measure the performance improvements without a thorough test plan.

Basically, compression enables more rows to be stored per physical block, which results in less overall blocks to store the data. In turn, this means less work is required during a query operation. Disk I/O is further reduced because the compressed values are more likely to be memory resident and don't require disk access. Compression is great for full table scan operations, and any extra CPU utilization for these efforts is negligible in today's Teradata systems.

> *Tip* - Another excellent approach involves compressing small tables so that it's possible to fit the whole table into spool or memory for improved query processing.

The best candidates for compression are fixed-width columns with a small number of frequently occurring values. Even though these column characteristics are for the very best candidates, you may choose to compress other columns just to save space. This is perfectly legitimate.

Here are some general rules and facts about compression:

- Only fixed width columns can be compressed at present.
- Up to 255 values can be compressed per column, including NULL values.
- 255 bytes is the maximum size of a compress value.
- 510 bytes is the maximum for character set Unicode.
- You can't compress primary index columns.
- You can't compress volatile or derived table columns.
- You can't compress referencing foreign key columns including soft RI. However, with Teradata Version 12, this is supported
- Nulls are automatically compressed when the COMPRESS clause is assigned.
- There is also an 8192 byte/character limit for the entire list of compressed items.
- Compression is case sensitive.

Starting with V2R6.1.x, the data rows now remain compressed in spool so that the cache can hold more logical rows.

When compression is carried over to spool files, only the compressed bits are copied. This works just like it does for normal tables and saves both CPU and I/O. Compression values are stored in the table header while the spool file is being processed. This process will be explained later on in this chapter.

How Compression Works

Compression values are defined at the column level. Therefore, the CREATE/ALTER (DDL) table statement is used to identify what values in each column will be compressed. When implemented, compressed values are moved out of the row and stored in the table header once. No matter how many times this value repeats itself at the row level, it is only stored once in the table header.

The first 14 bytes of every table row header is reserved for overhead. Presence bytes are used for both nullability and compression. An extra presence bit is needed when a column is defined as nullable. Even if there is no compression defined on the column, one presence bit will be required if the column is defined as nullable. If a null value is stored in this non-compressed and nullable column, then the presence bit will contain a 0.

Teradata uses the binary interpretation of the presence bits to index the compression values. Any values that are not compressed and NOT NULL will have all zeroes for their presence bits. If the column is defined as nullable, then compressible values will start with a leading 0 presence bit and will contain at least one 1 in the rest of the presence bits. Values that don't get compressed will start with a 1 as the leading presence bit, and the rest of its presence bits will be 0.

The example below shows a table that has compression on the Dept_No column. This column is also defined to allow for NULL values because the NOT NULL has not been specified.

```
CREATE SET TABLE csql_class.employee_table_comprx
  (
   Employee_No INTEGER,
   Last_name CHAR(20),
   First_name VARCHAR(12),
   Salary DECIMAL(8,2),
   Dept_No SMALLINT COMPRESS (200, 300,400,500))
UNIQUE PRIMARY INDEX ( Employee_No )
INDEX (DEPT_NO);
```

The illustration below demonstrates how presence bit patterns are defined on the compressed table. Notice that values with leading "0's" followed by a combination of "0's" and "1's" are compressed. Also, values with leading "1's" followed by all "0's" are not compressed in the table row header. In addition, note that the NULL's are represented by all "0's". The leading "0" or "1" indicates that the column is nullable. This leading bit would not be required if the column was not NULL.

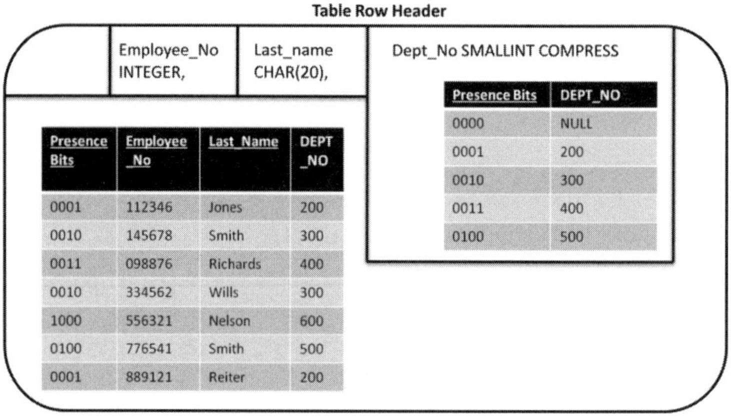

Table Row Header

	Employee_No INTEGER,	Last_name CHAR(20),	Dept_No SMALLINT COMPRESS

Presence Bits	DEPT_NO
0000	NULL
0001	200
0010	300
0011	400
0100	500

Presence Bits	Employee _No	Last_Name	DEPT _NO
0001	112346	Jones	200
0010	145678	Smith	300
0011	098876	Richards	400
0010	334562	Wills	300
1000	556321	Nelson	600
0100	776541	Smith	500
0001	889121	Reiter	200

As you can see, all the combinations of bit patterns are used to identify and locate the values. In this example, the bit patterns and their corresponding values are listed below:

- 0000-Rows that are NULL's

- 0001-Dept_No 200 is compressed in the table header
- 0010-Dept_No 300 is compressed in the table header
- 0011-Dept_No 400 is compressed in the table header
- 0100-Dept_No 500 is compressed in the table header
- 1000-Dept_NO 600 is NOT compressed in the table header

In this case, there are 5 potential values for compression (NULL, 200, 300, 400, 500), which requires 4 bits because the column is nullable. These values will be stored in the table row header. However, only Dept_No 600 will be stored in the base row.

Determining the Table Header size

To determine how much table header size is being taken up by compression, you can get a rough idea by creating two tables, one with compression and one without. Leaving both tables empty, query the catalog with the following query:

```
SEL TableName,CurrentPerm
FROM DBC.TableSize
WHERE DatabaseName = 'CSQL_CLASS'
AND TableName in
('Customer_table_Compressed','Customer_table');
```

The above query will return a single row for each table and for every AMP on the system. This is because table header information, or CREATE TABLE definition, is stored on all AMPs. Even if an AMP has no rows located on it, they will still have the compressed values stored in the table header. With this approach, it is actually possible to use more space with compression turned on. However, if each AMP contains the compressed value at least once, then compression should be saving space. As the frequency of the values increase in the table, the space savings increases proportionately.

Lastly, since the compressed values are stored in table header row, the CREATE/ALTER statement will fail if adding the compress values for a column causes the table row header to exceed 128K, which is the maximum size as of V2R6.x. Starting with Teradata Version 13, the maximum size of the row header is 1MB.

Considerations before implementing compression

Before implementing compression, make sure you consider possible alternatives first. There are several techniques that can save space before compression is implemented. For example, make sure your data types are as narrow as possible first. This will save space before compression is applied.

In order to do this correctly, you need to know how many bytes are taken up by each data type and implement them as efficiently as possible. For example, if you code INTEGER for a column that never contains values greater than 100, then you are wasting space. Integers use up 4 bytes. Utilizing a BYTEINT instead for this column would have sufficed and only used up a single byte. When applied, these techniques can provide significant space savings before the implementation of compression.

> Tip - Don't ever code VARCHAR(1) as a data type.

Take note that VARCHAR uses two bytes for every column and every row. Actually, the first VARCHAR column in the CREATE TABLE statement uses four bytes of overhead, and every VARCHAR in the row after that consumes two bytes just for overhead. Therefore, don't ever code VARCHAR(1) as a data type. CHAR(1) will always use less space. This is true if you define compression on this column or not. Considerable space savings may be gained simply by changing VARCHAR to CHAR for certain columns.

Determining the proper Data Type

As noted previously, make sure you have the most efficient field widths first. The following SQL or function (TYPE) demonstrates how to determine the correct data type. Perform the following function call on the maximum value expected for a given column.

```
sel  type(102.98);

Answer:  DECIMAL(5,2)

sel type(10998);

Answer:  SMALLINT
```

Implementing Compression

After you identify the list of compressed values for each column, then you define these values in the CREATE TABLE statement. You can implement compression when you create the table with the CREATE statement, or in some cases, with the ALTER table statement. Here is an example of the syntax on Dept_No:

```
CREATE SET TABLE csql_class.employee_table_new
   (
    Employee_No INTEGER,
    Last_name CHAR(20),
    First_name VARCHAR(12),
    Salary DECIMAL(8,2),
    Dept_No SMALLINT COMPRESS (200, 300,400,500,600))
UNIQUE PRIMARY INDEX ( Employee_No )
INDEX (DEPT_NO);
```

Compression savings are a function of the number of values compressed, the frequency that those values appear in the table and the field width. Table header limits are more easily reached when the fields are wider. Therefore, you will want to take the Top N values for these wider columns. This may be desired for other columns as well just to maintain the readability of the DDL.

Tip - Although you can compress up to 255 values per column, you may choose not to either because the optimal number of values is less or you want to maintain more readable DDL.

We mentioned that you can compress up to 255 values per column, but that doesn't mean you should. Typically, the number of optimal column values to compress is less than 255 values. This is based on the data that is stored in the table. In addition, you may choose to compress lesser values in order to maintain the readability of the DDL, which might be an important consideration when implementing compression.

Another best practice when optimizing value compression is to ensure column values do not exceed the size of the row header maximum size. Keep the number of values within these boundaries (1, 3, 7, 15, 31, 63, 127, or 255) because these numbers of values will not require additional presence bits in the row header. However, if you have enough columns that use additional presence bit(s), eventually this will require a longer row header. In this case, lesser is sometimes better if it does not require additional presence bytes, so you may need to test different scenarios.

Compression Case Sensitivity Example

We also mentioned that compression is case sensitive even though Teradata, by default, is not. This requires a work-around when data being inserted is of mixed case. The following example will shed some light on this issue.

```
CREATE SET TABLE csql_class.employee_table
   (
    Employee_No INTEGER,
    Last_name CHAR(20) COMPRESS 'Flintstone',
    First_name VARCHAR(12),
    Salary DECIMAL(8,2),
    Dept_No SMALLINT COMPRESS (200, 300,400,500,600))
UNIQUE PRIMARY INDEX ( Employee_No )
INDEX (DEPT_NO);
```

In this example, we are now compressing Last_name for values of 'Flintstone'. However, if 'FLINTSTONE' is inserted into the table, compression will not take place. This is fixed with the UPPERCASE keyword as the following syntax illustrates:

```
Last_name CHAR(20) COMPRESS 'FLINTSTONE' UPPERCASE,
```

This will now compress both 'Flintstone' and 'FLINTSTONE' or any other combination of upper and lower case when rows are inserted into the table because it is forced to upper case. The downside of this alternative is that all values will get returned as UPPERCASE when retrieved.

How to identify Multi-Value Column Candidates for Compression

This procedure enables you to identify the top 255 multi-value candidates for each column in a table. The entire code for this stored procedure (COMPRESSION_ANALYZER) can be found in Appendix E.

```
REPLACE PROCEDURE CSQL_PROC.COMPRESSION_ANALYZER
(
  IN   DB_IN     VARCHAR(60),      -- DatabaseName
  IN   TAB_IN    VARCHAR(60),      -- TableName
  OUT  Orc       INTEGER,          -- Return Code
  OUT  Omsg      VARCHAR(10000)    -- Output message
)
BEGIN
```

This procedure begins with the CREATE or REPLACE PROCEDURE statement followed by the procedure name. Input and Output parameters are also specified within the parenthesis. It is important to know that Output parameters can be set within the body of the stored procedure, but they cannot be referenced.

This program will ask for two input parameters, first being the database name and the second is the table name that will be analyzed for value compression candidates.

The following excerpt of this stored procedure identifies the 255 multi-value candidates for each column on the table that was defined by the input variables on the previous page.

```
-- Analyze each column in the table
SET PriorStmt='Open ColCurs for first time.';
OPEN ColCurs;
FETCH ColCurs INTO FieldNm,MaxL;
-- CursCnt prevents infinite loop
WHILE (SQLCODE=0) AND (CursCnt < 10000) DO
      SET UpperLimit = .125 / CAST(MaxL AS DECIMAL(25,3));
      SET Stmt = ' INS INTO CSQL_CLASS.COMP_ANALYSIS
               SEL '''||TRIM(DB_IN)||''','''||TRIM(TAB_IN)||''',
                 '''||TRIM(FieldNm)||''',
                 CAST(ColValue AS VARCHAR(32767)),
                 VAL_CNT,Frequency,CURRENT_DATE
               FROM (SEL '||TRIM(FieldNm)||' AS ColValue
                 ,CAST(COUNT(*) AS DECIMAL(25,3)) as VAL_CNT
                 ,VAL_CNT/'||CAST(Cntr AS VARCHAR(25))||' AS Frequency
                  FROM '||FullTabNm||'
                  GROUP BY 1
                  HAVING Frequency>'||CAST(UpperLimit AS VARCHAR(25))||') a
               QUALIFY row_number() over (ORDER BY VAL_CNT DESC ) <= 255;';
      CALL DBC.SysExecSQL(:Stmt);
      SET CursCnt = CursCnt+1;
      FETCH ColCurs INTO FieldNm,MaxL;
END WHILE;
CLOSE ColCurs;
END;
```

Alter Options with Compression

You can add a new column with multi-value compression to an existing table, add multi-value compression to an existing column, or drop compression from an existing column through the ALTER TABLE command. Compression can be dropped from a column by specifying the NO COMPRESS attribute. If a column is constrained as NOT NULL, then none of the specifications in the compression list can contain the literal NULL.

The ALTER TABLE COMPRESS syntax supports the following:

- Both populated and empty tables
- Global Temporary tables
- Base table columns where join indexes are defined
- Base table columns where hash indexes are defined

To ALTER a table in order to add compression columns, use the ALTER TABLE option as shown below:

```
ALTER TABLE CSQL_CLASS.Employee_Table
ADD SSN COMPRESS (612,803, 770),
ADD gender_code COMPRESS ('Female','Male'),
ADD job_desc COMPRESS ('Programmer','Manager');
```

Starting with V2R6.2, the ALTER statement can now compress populated columns. This is implemented by using the ALTER TABLE MODIFY option as shown below.

```
ALTER TABLE CSQL_CLASS.Employee_Table
MODIFY dept_no
COMPRESS (200, 300,400,500,600,700,800);
```

Take note that this command will enforce an exclusive lock on the table for the entire duration of the command. This could have a significant impact if the table is large because users will be unable to read or write to this table while this compress operation is taking place. Therefore, if you are working with large tables, it is recommended that you do these types of operations during off-hours.

Multi-Value Compression vs. VARCHAR

An alternative to compression is utilizing the VARCHAR(N) data type. In contrast to a fixed-length CHAR data type, the VARCHAR length consists of the data plus 2 bytes. The (N) bytes per row represent the actual number of characters in each individual field if fully populated.

Note: For certain character types like character set Unicode, there are 2*N bytes.

Analyzing the data demographics can assist you in determining whether a VARCHAR data type is more efficient than a CHAR fixed length data type with compression. The key important factors consist of the following:

- The maximum length of the field
- The average length of the field
- How compressible the field is – in other words, the field better have a significant number of repeating values

So the question is which is better, VARCHAR vs. Compression? Use the following guidelines to make this determination.

1. VARCHAR is more efficient when the difference of the maximum and average field length is high and data value compression or compressibility is low.
2. The combination of Compression and CHAR data types is more efficient when the difference of the maximum and average field length is low and the ability to compress is high.
3. When neither option above provides a clear advantage, the recommendation is to use VARCHAR because it uses somewhat less CPU resources.

Special Note: As of Teradata 13.10, value list compression will also support VARCHAR, and CHAR(>255) data types.

Compression Considerations

Use the following chart to make determinations on what data types are supported or not as of Teradata Version 12.

Supported	Not Supported
BYTE (max of 255 bytes)	Identity
BYTEINT	VARCHAR
CHAR (max of 255 characters)	LONG VARCHAR
DATE	VARGRAPHIC
DECIMAL/NUMERIC	VARBYTE
DOUBLE PRECISION	BLOB
FLOAT	CLOB
INTEGER	
REAL	
SMALLINT	

The following rules apply when adding or modifying rows with compression:

1. For single-value compression, the default for the compress value is NULL.
2. There is no default for multi-value compression. All values in the compression list must be specified explicitly.
3. NULL does not need to be specified in a multi-value compression statement. If there is a COMPRESS clause, NULL is compressed automatically.
4. You can modify an existing column to have multi-value compression.
5. You cannot add a compress value to a column if the table header row exceeds its maximum length of 128KB for V2R6.x, and 1MB for Teradata Version 13.

You should not compress columns where NULL values are subject to change. If NULL values change, the column will expand and you could cause block splits. Additional considerations include:

- Adding a column that is not compressible will most likely expand all rows.
- Adding a column that is compressible where there are no spare presence bits will expand the row size.
- Nullable fields also require a presence bit, even if it is not compressible. Therefore, if there are no spare presence bits, the row header and each row will expand.
- Dropping a column changes all row sizes where data is present.

Summary

Implementing compression correctly can improve performance and save significant space on your system. Saving space and resources translates into dollar savings and possibly preventing premature or unnecessary hardware upgrades.

You should evaluate alternatives such as data type resizing before implementing compression for a particular column(s). However, if the decision is made to implement multi-value compression, it is recommended that you optimize it for 1, 3, 7, 15, 31, 63, 127, or 255 numbers of values. Also, be mindful of NULLs and how they compress.

Lastly, measure the space and performance gains that you make with multi-value compression, and report these results to the appropriate management levels.

Chapter 11 - DBA Tricks of the Trade

Automation
Dynamic SQL
Stored Procedures
Macros

Little tricks can help us all be much more efficient. Get to know the tools and applications that are available and use them to the fullest. This chapter will site a few examples that are not commonly known, but can enhance productivity.

We mentioned earlier the importance of automation. In order to automate effectively, proficiency must be acquired with general SQL, Macros, Stored Procedures and dynamic SQL. Most repetitive tasks can be automated to some degree, if not completely. Make the investment early-on by automating processes, and the pay-off will be immediately recognized.

Automation Examples

Dynamic SQL is probably the best weapon when it comes to automation and efficiency. Consider querying the Data Dictionary (or DBC) to create final SQL, DML or DDL scripts whenever bulk commands are needed. Here are some examples of such queries.

Dynamic Query Example #1

```
SELECT 'CT  <DATABASE2>.'||TRIM(TABLENAME)|| ' AS  '||
TRIM(DATABASENAME)||'.'||TRIM(TABLENAME)||'  WITH  NO DATA;' (TITLE '')
FROM DBC.TABLES
WHERE DATABASENAME = '<TARGET DATABASE>'
ORDER BY TABLENAME;
```

Dynamic Query Example #2

```
SELECT 'ALTER TABLE ' ||TRIM(DATABASENAME)||'.' ||TRIM(TABLENAME) ||'
ADD OP_INS_BY  CHAR(6) COMPRESS,
ADD OP_INS_TS  TIMESTAMP(6) COMPRESS,
ADD OP_UPD_BY  CHAR(6) COMPRESS,
ADD OP_UPD_TS  TIMESTAMP(6) COMPRESS;
 ' (TITLE '')
FROM DBC.TABLES
WHERE TRIM(DATABASENAME) = '<TARGET DATABASE>'
ORDER BY DATABASENAME. TABLENAME:
```

These examples are trivial, but demonstrate the basic dynamic generation functionality. The goal is to minimize manual operations and eliminate mistakes brought on by these manual efforts. The more that is automated, the more time a DBA has to be proactive rather than reactive.

Using Macros

Macros are limited in functionality, yet they are extremely useful. Once standards and conventions for DDL are established, macros can be developed to analyze DDL against these standards. Macros can also be used to identify reserved words, build base and application views, run reports, perform maintenance, and much more.

Macros are very helpful for such activities as multi-statement processing and definitely have their place, but they also have some major limitations. For example, data definition statements are allowed in macros only if they are the only SQL statement in the macro. This makes it impossible to perform simple operations like dropping and recreating an object within a single macro. The parameters that can be passed into macros are also limited to data values. Database and object names are not valid macro parameters. Stored procedures work great, but definitely require more programming skills.

Macro Example to Create View Definitions

The following macro generates DDL to create basic views that will target either tables or other views. This macro is intelligent enough to put ACCESS LOCKS on the table if the target is actually a table.

```
REPLACE MACRO ViewCreate (VIEWDB CHAR(30), DB CHAR(30), TB CHAR(30))
/* Enter Database where views will be created as VIEWDB first.
  Enter Target Database where tables or base views reside as DB, and target Table
name as TB in quotes.
  Example:  Exec  ViewCreate ('View_DB', 'TAB_DB', 'TAB_NM');   */
AS
(SELECT colnm  (Title ' ') FROM (
SELECT DISTINCT '1' linenum, 9999 colid, 'REPLACE VIEW
'||TRIM(:VIEWDB)||'.'||TRIM(TableName)||' (' (VARCHAR(150)) colnm
FROM DBC.Columns
WHERE DatabaseName = :DB AND TableName = :TB
UNION
SELECT  '2' linenum, ColumnId,
      TRIM(ColumnName)||CASE WHEN ColumnId = MAX(ColumnId)
                                    OVER (PARTITION BY DatabaseName,TableName)
                              THEN ' ' ELSE ','
                              END AS colnm
FROM DBC.Columns
WHERE DatabaseName = :DB AND TableName = :TB
UNION
SELECT DISTINCT '3'  linenum,  9999 colid,
          CASE WHEN TableKind = 'T'     -- If Table, then Access Lock
                THEN ') AS LOCKING
'||TRIM(DatabaseName)||'.'||TRIM(TableName)||' FOR ACCESS SELECT '
                ELSE ') AS  SELECT '
          END AS colnm
FROM DBC.Tables
WHERE DatabaseName = :DB AND TableName = :TB
UNION
SELECT  '4' linenum, ColumnId,
      TRIM(ColumnName)||CASE WHEN ColumnId = MAX(ColumnId)
                                    OVER (PARTITION BY DatabaseName,TableName)
                              THEN ' ' ELSE ','
                              END AS colnm
FROM DBC.Columns
WHERE DatabaseName = :DB AND TableName = :TB
UNION
SELECT DISTINCT '5'  linenum, 9999 colid, 'FROM
'||TRIM(DatabaseName)||'.'||TRIM(TableName)||';'  colnm
FROM DBC.Columns
WHERE DatabaseName = :DB AND TableName = :TB
) f (linenum,colid,colnm)
ORDER BY linenum,colid;
);
```

Using Stored Procedures

The following stored procedure is worth several hundred times the price of this book just by itself.

Stored Procedure Example to Create Views

This procedure generates view DDL as the macro above, but it also executes it when instructed. This stored procedure is quite efficient and can be called by another procedure or macro to generate views for an entire database, or just for any tables or views that have changed in a given database. No DBA should be without such automation. It eliminates mistakes made by manual intervention, and provides the ability to fully automate changes into production and development. The stored procedure is illustrated in full on the following pages.

```
REPLACE PROCEDURE  CRE_BASE_V  (
  IN    V_DB                  VARCHAR(60),
  IN    T_DB                  VARCHAR(60),
  IN    TAB_NM                VARCHAR(60),
  IN    EX_DDL                CHAR(1),
  OUT  Omsg                   VARCHAR(10000)
)
BEGIN

/*
Program Designer:  Your Name          Date: March 2, 2009

Important facts:
   --  Until V12, must be owner  to compile  - dynamic SQL
   --  Owner - SELECT granted on DBC with GRANT OPTION; */

 /*  Variable Declaration Section*/
DECLARE RetCd             VARCHAR(10)  Default '99';
DECLARE Stmt              VARCHAR(10000);
DECLARE CursCnt           INTEGER        Default 0;
DECLARE ColNm             VARCHAR(100)  Default Null;
DECLARE CurTabTyp         CHAR(1)   Default Null;
DECLARE PriorStmt         VARCHAR(10000) Default Not set';

/*  Cursor Declaration Section*/
DECLARE   ColCurs        SCROLL CURSOR FOR
SELECT TRIM(ColumnName)||
          CASE WHEN columnid = MAX(ColumnId)
               OVER (PARTITION BY databasename,tablename)
                 THEN ' ' ELSE ',' END ||'0D0A'xc
FROM  DBC.Columns
WHERE DataBaseName = ''|| :T_DB || ''
AND  TableName = ''|| :TAB_NM || ''
ORDER BY ColumnId;
/* Procedure Section */
Lab1:  BEGIN
DECLARE EXIT HANDLER FOR SQLEXCEPTION
Begin
   SET RetCd=SQLCODE;
   SET Omsg='SQL ERROR -  '|| RetCd ||'  Executed following:  '|| PriorStmt;
End;
```

<Continued on Next Page>

<Continued>

```
/* Input parameter Validation Section*/

/*If  view database name is null , then end with error*/
IF (V_DB = '') or (V_DB is Null)  or (TRIM(V_DB) is Null)
THEN
   SET Omsg='ERROR 31- No View Database Name was entered as First Parameter!';
   SET RetCd='31';
   LEAVE Lab1;
END IF;
             <Validate rest of Input parameters here.>

/*  Validate Table existence and get Tablekind
  Log on as  procedure owner and have DBC Select access*/
SET PriorStmt='SELECT  TableKind  INTO ...   to get Table Kind';
SELECT  TableKind  INTO :CurTabTyp
FROM  DBC.Tables
WHERE  DatabaseName = ''|| trim(:T_DB) || ''  and TABLENAME =  ''|| trim(:TAB_NM) ||
'';

 IF CurTabTyp IS NULL
THEN
   SET Omsg='ERROR 35 - Table not found in Database!  ' || upper(trim(T_DB))
||'.'||upper(trim(TAB_NM));
   SET RetCd='35';
   LEAVE Lab1;
END IF;

/* Start building CREATE VIEW DDL  */
SET Stmt = 'REPLACE VIEW '|| UPPER(TRIM(V_DB))  ||'.'|| UPPER(TRIM(TAB_NM)) ||
' ( ' ||'0D0A'xc;

SET PriorStmt='Open ColCurs for first time.';
OPEN ColCurs;
FETCH ColCurs INTO ColNm ;
-- CursCnt prevents infinite loop
WHILE (SQLCODE=0) AND (CursCnt < 10000) DO
    SET Stmt = Stmt ||trim(ColNm) ;
    SET CursCnt = CursCnt+1;
    FETCH ColCurs INTO ColNm ;
END WHILE;
CLOSE ColCurs;
```

<Continued on Next Page>

```
<Continued>

-- Put ACCESS LOCKING in view if Target is a Table
IF UPPER(CurTabTyp) = 'T'
THEN
   SET Stmt = Stmt || ') AS LOCKING  '|| UPPER(TRIM(T_DB))  ||'.'||
UPPER(TRIM(TAB_NM)) || '  FOR ACCESS SELECT '  ||'0D0A'xc;
ELSE
   SET Stmt = Stmt || ') AS  SELECT '  ||'0D0A'xc;
END IF;

SET PriorStmt='Open ColCurs for Second time.';
OPEN ColCurs;
FETCH ColCurs INTO ColNm ;
-- CursCnt will prevent an infinite loop
WHILE (SQLCODE=0) AND (CursCnt < 10000) DO
    SET  Stmt = Stmt ||trim(ColNm) ;
    SET CursCnt = CursCnt+1;
    FETCH ColCurs INTO ColNm ;
END WHILE;
CLOSE ColCurs;

SET Stmt = Stmt || 'FROM  '|| UPPER(TRIM(T_DB))  ||'.'|| UPPER(TRIM(TAB_NM)) || '; '
;

SET Omsg=Stmt;

-- If  EX_DDL = 'Y',  create the view in the db.  Else will fail.
IF UPPER(EX_DDL) = 'Y'
THEN
   SET PriorStmt=Stmt;
   CALL DBC.SysExecSQL (:Stmt);
   SET Omsg='-- View Definition for: ' || upper(trim(V_DB))  ||'.'|| upper(trim(TAB_NM)) ||
'0D0A'xc||Stmt;
END IF;

END Lab1;
END;
```

This stored procedure can be called from a command line or another stored procedure as such:

```
CALL CRE_BASE_V('ViewDB','TargetDB','TabNm','Y',Omsg) ;
```

The fourth parameter instructs the stored procedure to run the DDL after it creates it. Otherwise, it will just display the DDL in the output parameter Omsg. When the Omsg output is copied back to the SQL Assistant query window, it will be displayed correctly. BTEQ will not display the DDL neatly, but it will create and execute the DDL fine.

A Teradata Administrator Trick

Here is a simple little adjustment that can be made to Teradata Administrator's definition file that may turn out quite useful. This illustration is practical in that it enhances the current Table Space report, but more importantly, it demonstrates the capability for customizing reports to one's own preferences. Let's cut to the chase.

The Table Space report in Teradata Administrator is activated by right-clicking on any database, and selecting "Table Space report." However, as the following illustration reveals, the creator name for the objects is lost and no longer available as it is when the list of objects in a database is displayed.

Default Table Space Report

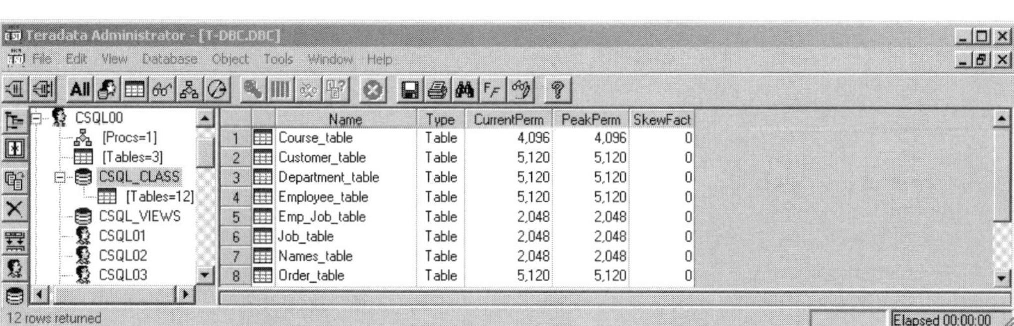

The table space report is particularly useful in determining space hogs and identifying which users are causing skewing in a particular database. Once tables are identified as problematic, then you have to double-click on the database again or List All Objects again and scroll to that object to see who the creator is. This becomes tedious and time consuming if there are numerous tables that need identifying.

Altering the Table Space Report

The following example alters the Table Space report to include the creator name and comment string for each object. This takes only a few minutes to set up, but the future time saved is well worth it. So, how is this done?

Teradata Administrator uses a definition file called winddi.def, which is found in the *sql* directory under the Teradata Administrator installation directory. The default installation directory is *C:\Program Files\NCR\Teradata Administrator V.X\SQL*. This file needs to be edited, but make a backup copy of it first.

Using notepad, edit the winddi.def file as such. Search for a line starting with "S9=", but it has to be under the correct version of the database. The versions are sectioned off within the file. This line contains the SQL we will be modifying in order to add our two new columns. For purposes of readability, we have modified the following query on to separate lines, but this needs to be left all on the same line without a semicolon at the end in the winddi.def file.

Modified S9 Query - Version 6.2

```
Lock Dbc.TableSize for Access
SELECT " (Title "),TS.TableName AS Name,
'T' AS "Type",
SUM(TS.CurrentPerm) AS CurrentPerm,
SUM(TS.PeakPerm) AS PeakPerm,
(100 - (AVG(TS.CurrentPerm)/MAX(TS.CurrentPerm)*100)) AS SkewFactor,
" (Title "), T.CreatorName, T.CommentString
FROM Dbc.TableSize TS, Dbc.tables T
WHERE  T.tablename = TS.tablename
AND T.databasename = TS.databasename
AND TS.DataBaseName = ( ? (CHAR(30)))(NOT CS)
GROUP BY 2,7,8,9 ORDER BY 2
```

The query now joins to DBC.Tables, and there are actually three new columns added to the select list. A dummy column was added after the skew factor and before the CreatorName field. Although this is not desirable for the report, it is necessary due to the way Teradata Administrator processes the result. This is what the revised Table Space report looks like.

Revised Table Space Report

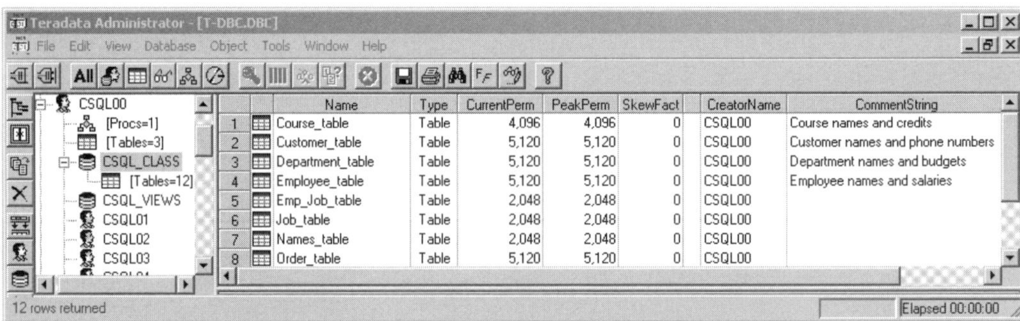

	Name	Type	CurrentPerm	PeakPerm	SkewFact		CreatorName	CommentString
1	Course_table	Table	4,096	4,096	0		CSQL00	Course names and credits
2	Customer_table	Table	5,120	5,120	0		CSQL00	Customer names and phone numbers
3	Department_table	Table	5,120	5,120	0		CSQL00	Department names and budgets
4	Employee_table	Table	5,120	5,120	0		CSQL00	Employee names and salaries
5	Emp_Job_table	Table	2,048	2,048	0		CSQL00	
6	Job_table	Table	2,048	2,048	0		CSQL00	
7	Names_table	Table	2,048	2,048	0		CSQL00	
8	Order_table	Table	5,120	5,120	0		CSQL00	

Shared code is used for several queries and several columns are assumed to be numeric. Therefore, any non-numeric fields will show up as 0. Columns can be hidden after by right-clicking on the heading and choosing "Hide Columns". However, this does not get saved within the application, so it needs to be done each time the application is brought up.

If "X" views are being used, then the winddix.def file must also be modified. In either case, the Teradata Administrator application will need to be restarted after the definition file is edited and saved.

Modified S9 Query - Version 12.0

Here is the Teradata 12.0 version of the same S9 query with the additional columns creator name and comment string.

```
S9=Lock Dbc.TableSizeV for Access
SELECT " (Title "),
S.TableName AS Name,T.TableKind AS "Type",
SUM(S.CurrentPerm) AS CurrentPerm,SUM(S.PeakPerm) AS PeakPerm,
(100 - (AVG(S.CurrentPerm)/MAX(S.CurrentPerm)*100)) AS SkewFactor,
" (Title "), T.CreatorName, T.CommentString
FROM Dbc.TableSizeV S, Dbc.TablesV T
WHERE S.DataBaseName=( ? (CHAR(30)))(NOT CS)
AND S.DataBaseName=T.DataBaseName
AND S.TableName=T.TableName
GROUP BY 2,3,8,9
ORDER BY 2
```

Using SQL Assistant

DBAs need to know the Teradata tools and applications to be as efficient as possible in their jobs. Take a few hours and get to know everything there is to know about tools like SQL Assistant and Teradata Administrator.

There is a lot more to SQL Assistant than just a place to run SQL. If taking a class is not possible, then just start with the manual or the Options and Help menu. Get to know the capabilities of each option so that time isn't wasted copying data to other programs or rerunning queries unnecessarily to perform simple aggregations, sorts, column reordering, column formatting, etc. Much of this can be done with SQL Assistant either by right-clicking in the answerset window, or with the tool bars that may need to be initiated under Tools→Customize, and then checking both the Answerset and Query check boxes. Or, right-clicking on any current tool bar and choosing Customize will accomplish the same thing.

The following illustrates show some of the important features to become familiar with. The Find Next, Replace, Uppercase buttons in the Query tool bar are absolutely irreplaceable, so get comfortable using them all.

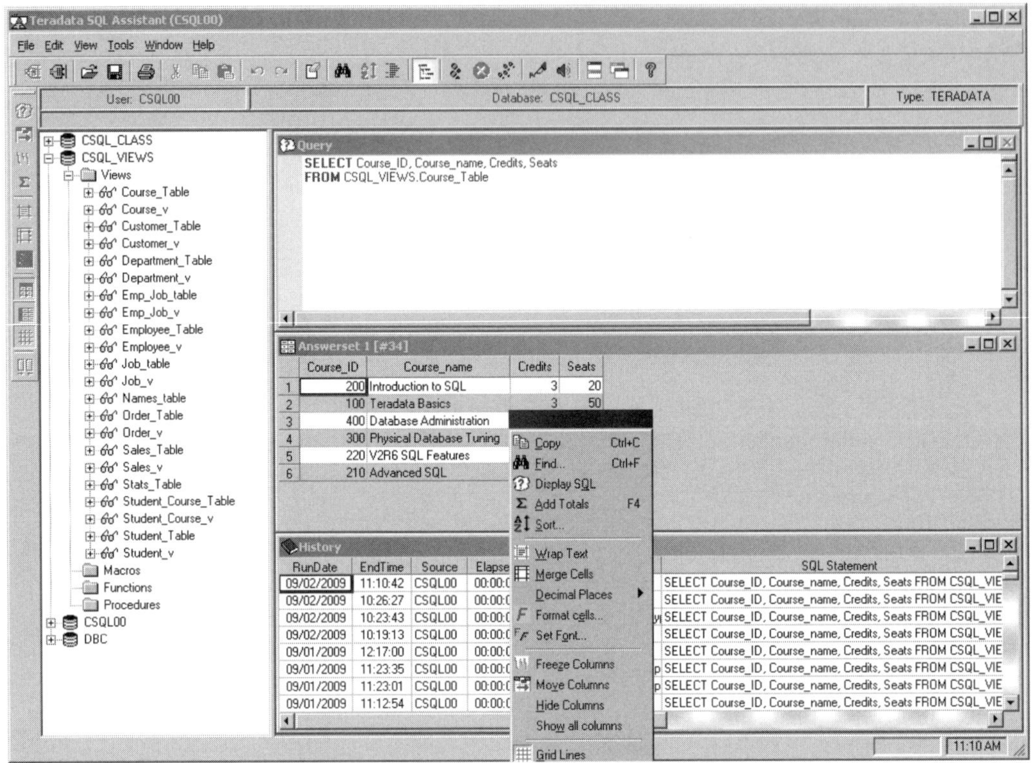

The typical location of the Tool bars for Teradata Administrator is at the top and left side of this window frame. However, these can be moved (or removed) where desired. The illustration on the previous page, we right-clicked on the answerset, which displays a multitude of options to choose from such as Add Totals, Sort..., Format Cells..., Freeze Columns, Move Columns, etc.

Without knowing what each of these do, it's tempting to copy all of the output to something like MS Excel and manipulate the data there. Or, many people will rerun the query specifying a different order or aggregation for the columns. Both of these may be unnecessary if all the options are well understood that are already provided with the tool.

Using Named Parameters

One very nice feature that often goes unnoticed is the ability to pass in Named Parameters into SQL. In order to make this work, make sure to check "Allow use of Named Parameters in queries" under Tools → Options → Query Tab. Now parameters can be passed into the SQL by prefixing the parameter name with a question mark as depicted in the SQL below (i.e. ?CredType)

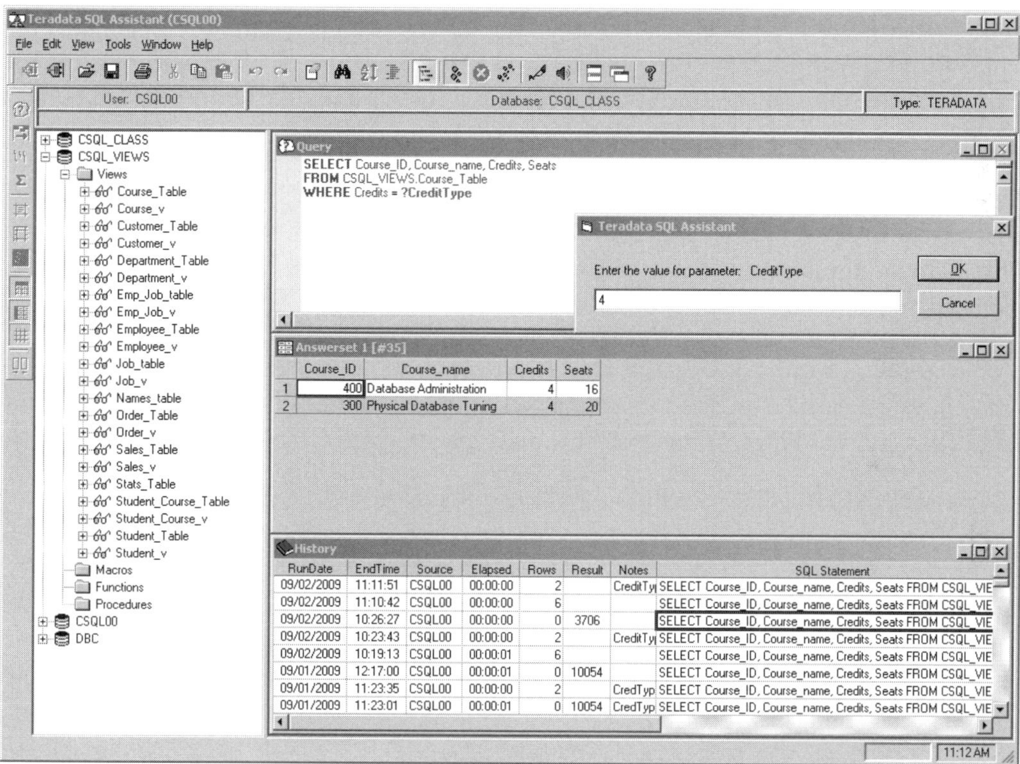

When this query is run, a message box will pop up asking for the value of the parameter CredType. We entered 4 in this example and those are the only two rows that were returned. This is very helpful when executing DDL across various development, test, and production databases. Take note also that the Tool Bars toggle in and out of activity depending on which section of SQL Assistant is currently active.

We suggest learning how to import and export results, drag and drop columns, objects and database names from the Explorer Tree to queries, schedule queries in Query Scheduler, and get to know the many options in the history window. For example, the Elapsed Time in the History window is equal to the Fetch Time plus the DBMS Time.

It also is important to know how much time is really spent running a query as opposed to how long it takes to move the data over the network. Also, double-clicking on a Result in the History window will display all of the errors for a given SQL script in one shot. A note can be assigned to any and all queries, and notes can even be prompted for every time a new query is executed.

We strongly suggest learning when to use each tool to improve overall productivity and efficiency. There are times to use SQL Assistant and there are times to use Teradata Administrator. Many DBAs get stuck on one tool, but there are definite benefits to each tool.

For example, to quickly check a row count on a table, check for indices, or check what statistics are collected on a table and when, then simply right click on the table in Teradata Administrator and select the action as such:

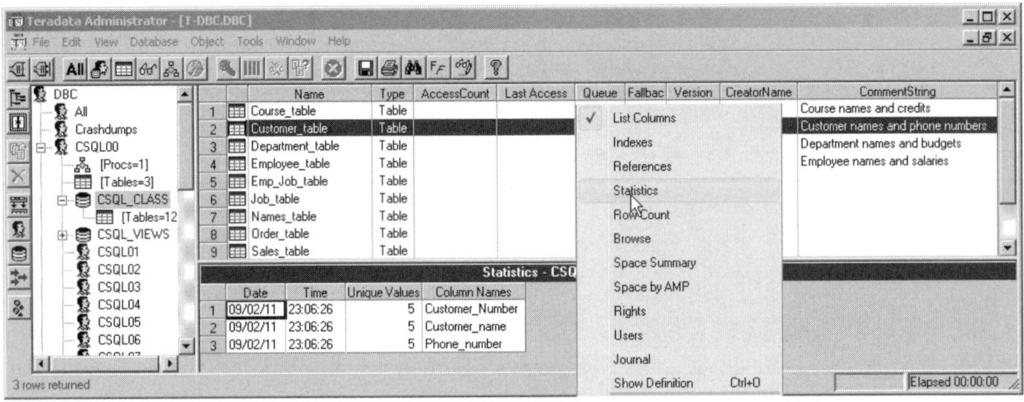

Use Teradata Administrator to quickly check the size of a table, get a list of columns, or check what rights exist on a table or database. Can these operations be performed using other tools? Sure, a separate HELP STATISTICS or SEL COUNT(*) command can be entered on every desired table in SQL ASSISTANT, etc., but why not use the tool that makes life easiest when its available?

Tools and Utilities Example

The purpose of this section is to demonstrate a single possibility. This will hopefully act as a starting point and open up opportunities for bigger and better solutions.

Shell Script to Move Data between Systems

The following example illustrates the use of UNIX shell scripting, BTEQ, FastExport, and MultiLoad to automate the movement of data from one Teradata system to another. This could just as well be accomplished through OleLoad, Perl, TPT, FastLoad, or other third-party tools. Here is the code followed by a brief description.

```
#!/bin/ksh
SOURCE_DB=$1
TARGET_DB=$2
TABLE_NAME=$3

# Makes provisions for tables greater than 27 characters.
if ((${#TABLE_NAME} >= 27))
then
  typeset -L27 WORK_TABLE=${TABLE_NAME}
else
  WORK_TABLE=${TABLE_NAME}
fi

# Remove and create pipe
rm -f ${TABLE_NAME}_P.OUT
mknod ${TABLE_NAME}_P.OUT p
```

<Continued Next Page>

<Continued>

```
run_exp()
{
fexp <<EOF
.LOGTABLE ${WORK_TABLE}L;
LOGON <TDP_ID>/<YOUR ID>,<YOUR_PASSWORD>;
DATABASE ${SOURCE_DB};

.BEGIN EXPORT SESSIONS 10;
.EXPORT OUTFILE ${TABLE_NAME}_P.OUT FORMAT FASTLOAD MODE
INDICATOR;

 select  * from ${TABLE_NAME};
.END EXPORT ;
.LOGOFF ;
EOF
}

# runs the prior function in batch mode while tables are cleaned
# up and MLOAD is initiated to load through a pipe
run_exp &

# BTEQ script cleans up work tables and releases mload.
# Errors goes to /dev/null, but can go elsewhere
bteq >>/dev/null <<EOF

.logon <TDP_ID of TARGET DB>/<YOUR ID>,<YOUR_PASSWORD>;
.set notify off
.set ERROROUT  STDOUT

.set errorlevel 3807 severity 0
.set errorlevel 2580 severity 0

release mload ${TARGET_DB}.${TABLE_NAME};
drop table userdb.WT_${WORK_TABLE};
drop table userdb.ET_${WORK_TABLE};
drop table userdb.UV_${WORK_TABLE};
drop table userdb.L_${WORK_TABLE};

.logoff;
.quit;
EOF
```

<Continued Next Page>

<Continued>

```
mload <<EOF

.LOGTABLE userdb.L_${WORK_TABLE};
.LOGON <TDP_ID>/<YOUR ID>,<YOUR_PASSWORD>;

DATABASE ${TARGET_DB};
.SET DBASE_TARGETTABLE TO '${TARGET_DB}';
.SET DBASE_WORKTABLE   TO '<YOUR WORK DB>';

delete from &DBASE_TARGETTABLE..${TABLE_NAME};

.BEGIN IMPORT MLOAD
      TABLES &DBASE_TARGETTABLE..${TABLE_NAME}
      WORKTABLES &DBASE_WORKTABLE..WT_${WORK_TABLE}
      ERRORTABLES &DBASE_WORKTABLE..ET_${WORK_TABLE}
      &DBASE_WORKTABLE..UV_${WORK_TABLE};
.
LAYOUT DATAIN_LAYOUT INDICATORS;
.TABLE &DBASE_TARGETTABLE..${TABLE_NAME};

.DML LABEL INSERT_DML;
    INSERT INTO &DBASE_TARGETTABLE..${TABLE_NAME}.*;

.IMPORT INFILE ${TABLE_NAME}_P.OUT
  FORMAT FASTLOAD
  LAYOUT DATAIN_LAYOUT
  APPLY INSERT_DML;

.END MLOAD;
.LOGOFF;
EOF

# Remove Pipe
rm -f ${TABLE_NAME}_P.OUT

exit
# End of shell
```

The comments in the shell script should help describe the process. It basically makes use of a named pipe to extract data via FastExport from one system and load it via MultiLoad to a table on another system. The program can certainly be made more elegant by accepting more parameters, creating the target table if it does not exist, or allowing the name of the target table to be changed.

This script was actually cut down for the sake of the illustration, and can be easily modified to make use of FastLoad, which will significantly improve performance. Even better performance can be obtained by using TPT, but the script would be dramatically changed and more complicated. The point of this illustration is to demonstrate that automation may require the knowledge and use of multiple disciplines in order to accomplish even the simplest of tasks.

Summary

We have just thrown a whole bunch of tidbits or tools out in one fairly short chapter. The purpose is to demonstrate easy ways to make the job more productive and easier in the long run.

We will continue to pour out more tools and tips throughout this book. No single book could possibly cover the endless possibilities and solutions for every situation or problem. Hopefully, some personal ideas and possibilities can be gleaned from this information. Much of the material presented in this chapter is to help get the ball rolling. There may be some time investment needed upfront, but the pay-off in the end is invaluable. As with any and all decisions, consult other individuals or companies that are already doing it.

Teradata representatives should be able to schedule some dialogues with other customers. Learn from their mistakes and successes, and see if they will even share some of their processes, procedures, documentation, or even code if necessary.

Chapter 12 – Canary Queries

Performance Automation Solution Reporting

Often overlooked, the Canary query may be the single-most important performance monitor and measurement tool in the toolbox. So where does the name "Canary query" come from? Even within the last century, coal miners would bring canaries into the mines to act as early detective signals for toxic gases such as carbon monoxide and methane. Being much more sensitive than human, the birds would get sick, giving the miners time to get out or put on protective respiratory equipment.

This is the same premise used for canary queries. A well established and static query is sent into the database on a frequent and set interval. If the query does not return or takes too long, then someone should be notified. It could be an indication that something is wrong or the system is really busy. Either way, the history must be kept for trending and monitoring overall performance over time. The canary queries provide a lot of insight into what the users are seeing on a daily basis.

There are differing views on how canary queries should be implemented. Teradata provides heartbeat queries as part of Teradata Manager and Viewpoint applications. These are great and provide a high level overview, but they only offer part of the picture.

Tip - Monitoring and alerting when a session takes too long to log in is more indicative of system problems than query response time.

This chapter discusses a homegrown approach, which will give more flexibility, paging and control. This process will also monitor the login duration as well, which is even more telling as to whether the database is having real problems or not. This approach is flexible enough to target any tables, which provides for a more realistic business perspective.

For example, if a load fails or statistics don't get collected correctly on an application table that is also part of the canary process, then the canary query will reflect the problem. This will alert the DBA to check the load and statistical collection process, hopefully before the users find it first. As just mentioned, this design also pages DBAs when either or both logons and run times are too long.

Building the Process

First, analyze your workload and select a consistent short running query that is representative of actual business user activity. It may be necessary to run this query many times on a quiescent system to get a baseline on its consistency. Although possible we don't suggest using a single-AMP or tactical query. Try to use an all-AMP or multi-AMP query to get a more realistic picture of what the users are seeing from a typical query.

Make a decision as whether to use DBQL or your own log table for capturing performance for these canaries. There are benefits to both methods, but a historical table is needed in either case. However, DBQL provides a lot more information than you can capture on your own. A good method may be a hybrid approach, where the DBQL information is captured in a historical table and used for reporting and trending. This is a much simpler method for coding.

The method proposed in this illustration focuses on capturing the canary results into a user defined log table. One thing DBQL doesn't do is capture the actual results of the query, which this proposed design can. If necessary for reporting, the DBQL information is always available as a compliment to the user defined log table.

In Teradata 12.0, you can tag the query for easier recognition via Query Banding, which is a method of naming or identifying the origin of a particular query. TASM can then adjust priorities accordingly or apply other workload management rules. DBQL will then log the query band tags for reporting purposes. However, putting a comment in the select clause or targeting the userid itself should suffice for canary reporting purposes.

The query band may be a better approach if just using DBQL to log query statistics. Just be careful not to modify or tune the workload management tool, like TASM, to give special assistance or resources to canary queries. These canary users need to be treated like every other user or their purpose is defeated.

The query should be embedded in a stored procedure like the following example below. The stored procedure inserts each row into the log table to signify the start of the query, runs the canary query, and then updates the log row with an end time stamp and results.

Canary Log Table Example

We used the KISS (Keep it simple Stupid) method in developing the next example to illustrate the process. We didn't address it in this example for simplicity sake, but consider running a similar or different canary query in each resource partition on the system.

This may provide a more realistic picture of overall system and workload performance. First, create a log table to house the results of the canary queries. This log table (i.e. CANARY_STATS) captures the query results as well, which may or may not be important to everyone. Sometimes, the right answer is just as important as the response time. DBQL will not capture the result, but it does return the number of rows returned, which may suffice.

Canary Log Table

```
CREATE SET TABLE CSQL_CLASS.CANARY_STATS (
    Q_NUM INTEGER,
    Q_BEGIN_TS TIMESTAMP(0),
    Q_END_TS TIMESTAMP(0),
    Q_ROWS INTEGER,
    Q_INFO VARCHAR(50),
    RUN_ID INTEGER)
PRIMARY INDEX (Q_NUM ,Q_BEGIN_TS);
```

Canary Procedure Example

This brings us to the stored procedure that updates this table and runs the canary query. Remember, stored procedures are not the only way to skin this cat, but they are flexible and allow for easy test executions from other applications, such as SQL Assistant and BTEQ.

Please note that input parameters are not necessary, but they are listed here for the example. The RUN_ID parameter does make it easier to run multiple canaries at the same time. This is a good idea to do from different Resource Partitions. The RUN_ID could signify a Resource Partition. Adding an output parameter for messages is a good idea, but again this is a simple example.

Simplified Canary Procedure Example

```
REPLACE PROCEDURE CSQL_PROC.CANARY_01
( IN  IN_DEPT  SMALLINT,
  IN  IN_RUN_ID  INTEGER)

BEGIN
DECLARE TMP_CNT INT;
DECLARE TMP_INFO VARCHAR(50);
DECLARE CUR_TM TIMESTAMP(0);

select CURRENT_TIMESTAMP(0) into :CUR_TM;

INS CSQL_CLASS.CANARY_STATS (1,:CUR_TM,NULL,NULL,NULL,:IN_RUN_ID);

SELECT  COUNT(*),'Canary 01 - 1-3 seconds'  INTO :TMP_CNT,:TMP_INFO
FROM
(SELECT DEPARTMENT_NAME
FROM CSQL_VIEWS.DEPARTMENT_TABLE
WHERE DEPT_NO >= :IN_DEPT) A;

UPDATE CSQL_CLASS.CANARY_STATS
  SET Q_END_TS = CURRENT_TIMESTAMP(0)
      ,Q_ROWS = :TMP_CNT
      ,Q_INFO = :TMP_INFO
 WHERE Q_NUM  =  1
  AND Q_END_TS IS NULL
  AND Q_BEGIN_TS = :CUR_TM
  AND Q_ROWS IS NULL
  AND Q_INFO IS NULL
  AND RUN_ID = :IN_RUN_ID;
END;
```

Canary Calling Shell Script

We have now addressed just part of the process. The real meat of this process is in the calling program. This program can be written in a variety of languages, such as SHELL or PERL. The following example will have excerpts of some shell scripts, and should be fairly straight-forward to follow. The trick to this program is to kick off a background process or shell script that does no more than logon to the database and call the canary procedure.

By making this a background process, someone can examine the displayed output from BTEQ and look for both a successful logon and execution of the procedure. Then alerts can be set for both the logon and the successful execution of the query. These alerts can be in the form of emails, pages, or both. Remember, alerting when logons take too long, is more indicative of a serious Teradata problem than a query taking too long.

Here is the shell script that logs in and calls the canary stored procedure. It doesn't get much simpler than this. $1 is a parameter that is passed in from calling program, and represents the logon string.

```
bteq <<EOF
.logon  $1

CALL CSQL_PROC.CANARY_01 (500,98);

.logoff;
.quit;
EOF
```

Canary Shell Script Extract

There is more to the calling program than what is listed below, but this is the foundation for the whole process. Every environment has its own process for mailing and paging from UNIX, so this part is left out. There are two main loops within this process. After the canary shell script above is initiated, the first WHILE loop continuously evaluates the output looking for a successful logon.

There is a sleep step of five seconds, which can be modified according to your preference. The program is looking for "*** Logon successfully completed" before the loop ends. After a preset number of iterations (or set amount of time), the program sends an email to the DBA group, and after a few more iterations, a page will go out.

The second loop takes place after a successful logon. Now we are looking for "*** Exiting BTEQ..." in order to assume the query or stored procedure finished gracefully. Again, a certain number of iterations will result in an email and a greater number of iterations will result in a page. There is a tuning effort that needs to take place here to determine what numbers to choose here. It also depends on the DBA's tolerance or threshold for paging.

the use of one anyway to maintain the security access for reporting, historical purposes, and possible auditing.

How does it work?

Instead of cross-joining to the USR_SEC control table to get an individual's security codes, the same information can be stored in the name of a Teradata profile, which can be accessed and parsed directly in the column select clause.

The join is eliminated completely. Again, we strongly suggest retaining and maintaining the user security table for reasons mentioned above. Other important reasons to keep the USR_SEC table as a control table is to automate the assignment of profiles to users across systems, restores, and to ensure the catalog is in sync with your control table.

The security codes are pulled out of the profile name via the SUBSTR function in the View definition. Assigned profile names can be accessed at the session level just like other options such as USER, DATE, CURRENT_TIME, DATABASE, ROLE, etc. with the PROFILE command.

SELECT PROFILE Example

```
SEL profile;

Profile

EMA
```

This would be an example of one such profile that gives full access to a user in our example. This user will be able to see every column. The first character from this profile name indicates the ability to see "Employee" data, the second allows access to "Manager" data, and the last character allows access to "Auditor" data.

Simple Profile Example

There is almost no overhead to this solution, and the performance is on par with accessing the table directly. The following example illustrates how this view definition now works. This is the same view as the last solution, but the profile is accessed and the join to the USR_SEC view is removed. Must create profiles for each possible combination of values. Since we have 3 possible values, then the number of profiles is 2 to the third power or 2*2*2 or 8.

The simple profile example below gives someone access to "Employee" and "Manager" data only. The "X" designates that the user cannot see Auditor data.

```
CREATE PROFILE EMX
  AS PASSWORD = (MINCHAR= 8);
```

More complicated Profile Example

This next profile is a bit more complicated and illustrates that the profiles can still be used as originally intended. However, as many combinations of each profile type are needed as the number of combinations of security codes. The user that gets assigned this profile will be able to see Manager and Auditor data, but will be blocked from seeing the Employee data. They will also get an account that will not expire, and will allow unlimited log on attempts, etc.

Create Profile Example

```
CREATE PROFILE XMA_NONEXPIRING
  AS PASSWORD = (MINCHAR= 8
                 ,EXPIRE = 0
                 ,MAXLOGONATTEMPTS = 0
                 ,LOCKEDUSEREXPIRE = 0
                 ,REUSE = 0);
```

Profile-Driven Masked Column View

```
REPLACE VIEW CSQL_VIEWS.CUST_TAB_SEC AS
SELECT
    C.CUST_NBR,
    C.CUST_NM,
    CASE WHEN C.SEC_CD = substr(profile,1,1)
            THEN C.PHONE_NBR
            WHEN C.SEC_CD = substr(profile,2,1)
            THEN C.PHONE_NBR
            WHEN C.SEC_CD = substr(profile,3,1)
            THEN C.PHONE_NBR
            ELSE '***********'
    END PHONE_NBR
FROM CSQL_VIEWS.CUST_TAB C;
```

Once the profiles are created and assigned to the appropriate users, then you can create the prior view to mask columns according to the profile assigned to the user accessing the view. Take note that row-level security columns are now compared to the parsed value from the profile name (i.e C.SEC_CD = substr(profile,1,1)).

Special Note: This solution assumes that there are not too many security code possibilities and the values that exist are not volatile. If there are too many security code combinations, then the number of profiles required may make the profile maintenance too cumbersome. The number of profiles already be in place may need to be considered before undertaking this strategy.

It is not desirable to have the number of possibilities ever-changing either. This will greatly detract from the flexibility and manageability of this solution.

One last possible solution is to create user defined functions to encrypt and decrypt columns rather than mask the columns with some dummy value. There are third-party vendors that will supply encryption algorithms as well. Rest-assured, there will be overhead, maintenance, and prices to pay with any chosen solution. Just make sure to choose a solution that meets business needs, and is also flexible and as easy as possible to manage.

Summary

The primary purpose of this chapter was to spark ideas and creativity. Several alternatives were mentioned for securing data, but you should choose a method that meets all your business needs and is as efficient and flexible as possible. This solution needs to be efficient and straight-forward for the administrators, architects, and users. The profile solution mentioned above for masking columns is truly worth paying attention to and understanding.

Chapter 14 - Performance Benchmark

Benchmark
Performance
Solution
Reporting

We sincerely advocate the institution of a performance benchmark process as well as a patch testing or regression testing process. A proper performance benchmark should be one of the first automation exercises. If migrating from another RDBMS to Teradata, then it's a good idea to automate a benchmark process even prior to the migration.

A comprehensive contract will include provisions for meeting certain performance benchmark results. Be sure that excessive tuning does not take place specifically to make the benchmark queries run faster. Take ownership of any benchmark process and be sure to oversee it from beginning to end.

Patch testing and regression testing will not be mentioned further, other than their importance should not go unrecognized and will require additional planning and automation. These are ever-changing and evolving test processes.

A really well written process should be flexible enough to run against multiple platforms or databases. Why is this important? It's imperative to have a way to measure exactly how well the Teradata system performs after a migration, upgrade, patch implementation, TASM implementation, or even certain major implementations, etc.

This needs to be a non-changing apples-to-apples comparison, so the following features need to be the same for every benchmark execution.

Characteristics of a Successful Benchmark

- Consistent and similar data being accessed
- Consistent indexing, views, security, priorities

- Queries represent a true mixed workload
- Maintains consistent concurrency levels
- Correct results captured every time
- Queries should be run in same order every time
- Same number of queries completed every time
- Meaningful reports

What does this all mean? The name of the game is consistency and non-volatility across each area. It would be optimal if enough space could be allocated so that the same volume of data, indexes, etc. was sliced off and maintained purely for the benchmark process. Data volumes increase, so if it is not possible to slice off a benchmark area, then make sure all other aspects are unchanging. For instance, account for changes in volumes as well as changes in the complexity of the environment.

Take note that project initiatives can cause significant impacts to benchmark results and trending. For example, the introduction of column masking or encryption in views can add significant overhead to query performance. Conversely, other project improvements may actually cause significant improvements in query performance. Either way, it will no longer allow for an apples-to-apples benchmark comparison over time, and may greatly impact trending analysis.

Due to this matter, the benchmark process should be executed before and after each major implementation to test the overall impact of such a change. If results do change dramatically, then run the benchmark at least three times to establish a new baseline. Someone needs to become intimately knowledgeable about the process as well as the environment at hand.

It is embarrassing to accuse a vendor that their software or hardware is not performing to expectations, only to find out that someone internally implemented a big change or load and forgot to recollect statistics or build some required Join Indexes.

It is very possible for queries to run much faster, longer, or not at all because of missing data, missing indexes or Join Indexes, missing statistics, and the possibilities go on and on. A report should be generated as soon as the last query **completes successfully**. Let's emphasize "completes successfully" because the benchmark is not done when the last query is submitted, but when it finishes. This means the external driving program needs to be smart enough to know when the last query finishes on the Teradata side of the house.

It will not suffice to just execute the benchmark and calculate the overall run time either. The results need to be captured and validated as well with every execution. The final reports should include an overall run time, results for each query type, how many times each ran, and the minimum, average and maximum duration of each query type. A nice-to-have report also lists the percent complete for each hour, which will indicate when a benchmark starts to get off track. It is amazing how consistent and reliable Teradata benchmarks can be given all things equivalent (i.e. unchanged quiescent system).

Our reference to concurrency above refers to number of simultaneous queries or sessions running at a time throughout the entire benchmark test. For example, the process may be designed to run 500 queries with 20 sessions running simultaneously throughout. Every time a query ends another one initiates, but never exceeds 20 at one time. This test then has a concurrency of 20. Maintaining a given concurrency is extremely important, but makes the automation much more challenging.

We offer one possible solution later, but there are many others. The queries need to be executed in the exact same order with each benchmark execution. A mixed workload refers to executing all different types of queries such as:

- Simple or short-running tactical queries (few seconds or less),
- Queries that run less than a minute, some that run several minutes
- Complex queries that run fairly long (20 minutes to an hour).

These queries should be representative of those executed by the user community, and the DBQL log tables are a great place to quickly capture these queries.

Building a Benchmark Solution

There are many languages and techniques that can be used to automate a benchmark process. The following illustration uses a combination of UNIX shell scripting and Teradata stored procedures, but this could certainly be accomplished in another language like Perl. Stored procedures may be avoided as well by simply using DBQL information. Using DBQL will be mildly touched on as the discussion continues.

> *Tip* - Capture the entire workload for the benchmark from the DBQL tables.

The first step is to capture a query workload that will be representative of real user activity. Simply query DBQL (namely DBC.QryLog and DBC.QryLogSQL) for queries that will meet the short, medium, and long requirements that were mentioned earlier. Identify a minimum of twenty to thirty queries that run consistently in as little as a few seconds, some that run under a minute, more that run in a few minutes, several minutes, and as long as an hour if need be.

Create Log Table

Every query should probably be altered to return a count as the final answer. That count can then be captured and stored in a log table by the stored procedure. Here is a suggestion for a simple log table below, followed by a simplified stored procedure to run a specific query.

Create Benchmark Log Table Example

```
CREATE SET TABLE CSQL_CLASS.BENCH_STATS
    (Q_NUM INTEGER,
     Q_BEGIN_TS TIMESTAMP(0),
     Q_END_TS TIMESTAMP(0),
     Q_ROWS INTEGER,
     Q_INFO VARCHAR(50),
     RUN_ID INTEGER)
PRIMARY INDEX BENCH_STATS_P (Q_NUM,Q_BEGIN_TS)
INDEX BENCH_STATS_S1 ( Q_NUM );
```

Simplified Stored Procedure Example

```
REPLACE PROCEDURE CSQL_PROC.BENCH_06
( IN  IN_DEPT  SMALLINT,
  IN  IN_RUN_ID  INTEGER)

BEGIN

DECLARE TMP_CNT INT;
DECLARE TMP_INFO VARCHAR(50);

INS CSQL_CLASS.BENCH_STATS
(6,CURRENT_TIMESTAMP(0),NULL,NULL,NULL,:IN_RUN_ID);

SELECT  COUNT(*), 'Query 6 -Tactical, 1-3 seconds' INTO :TMP_CNT,:TMP_INFO
FROM
(SELECT DEPARTMENT_NAME
FROM CSQL_VIEWS.DEPARTMENT_TABLE
WHERE DEPT_NO >= :IN_DEPT) A;

UPDATE CSQL_CLASS.BENCH_STATS
  SET Q_END_TS = CURRENT_TIMESTAMP(0)
      ,Q_ROWS = :TMP_CNT
      ,Q_INFO = :TMP_INFO
 WHERE Q_NUM  =  6
  AND Q_END_TS IS NULL
  AND Q_ROWS IS NULL
  AND Q_INFO IS NULL
  AND RUN_ID = :IN_RUN_ID;
END;
```

This stored procedure above is overly simplified, but does demonstrate some basics, such as passing in parameters, inserting into and updating a table and selecting multiple columns into multiple variables. It was kept simple for the sake of this illustration, but it would not hurt to add in some proper error handling, comments and more log information if necessary.

The Q_INFO column really is important because it tells information about the query type, which makes report diagnosis more straightforward and readable. In this procedure, we are reporting that this is a Tactical type query that should run within one to three seconds. If written well, a single stored procedure could probably handle all the different queries, but this may entail superfluous calls to the database, which could then affect the overall benchmark results.

This is where it may be possible to avoid using a stored procedure altogether by sending the output of the query to "/dev/null" on UNIX. Then the rows returned can be later retrieved from the *NumResultRows* column from DBC.QryLog.

Design queries not to return many rows, because network activity can affect benchmark results. Identifying and proving network bottlenecks as the cause of a poorly performing benchmark is very difficult after the fact. All other reporting and statistics can be mined out of the DBQL logs.

The Calling Program

The calling program (a shell script in this case) is obviously much larger than the following example, but this excerpt illustrates how to get the concurrency maintained throughout the program as well as how to call each stored procedure. There are number of shell parameters that are set prior to this section of code, but they should be fairly explanatory.

The concurrent processes are maintained by calling another short shell script and continuously checking that the number of related UNIX processes does not exceed the predefined concurrency threshold.

Extract from Benchmark Shell Script

This smaller shell script merely logs into Teradata and executes the stored procedure for the query. The SLEEP and WHILE commands are used to wait for a period of time before checking again and initiating another set of queries.

```
#/* Reads input file to get run order.
exec 5< ${HOMEDIR}/${RUN_ORDER_FILE}

while read -u5 Q_num
do
   #/*  Keep checking OS for benchmark and concurrency.
   c1=$(ps -fu ${UNIX_ID}|grep benchmark|grep -v grep|wc -l)
   if [ $c1 -gt ${CONCURRENCY} ]
   then
       #/* Loop sleeps 10 seconds before polling again.
       while [$(ps -fu ${UNIX_ID}|grep benchmark|grep -v grep|wc -l) -gt
       ${CONCURRENCY}]
       do
           sleep 10
       done
   fi
   Q_cnt=Q_cnt+1
   print $(date) ' - ' ${Q_num}' - ' ${Q_cnt} >>${LOGFI_2}
   ${HOMEDIR}/bench${Q_num}.sh ${Q_cnt} ${T_LOG} >>${LOGFI} &

done

#/* IMPORTANT - Loop checks to see when last query finally finishes.
#/* Prior loop finishes when last query is initiated.
while [ $(ps -fu ${UNIX_ID}|grep benchmark|grep -v grep|wc -l) -ge 2 ]
do
   #/* Sleep 5 seconds before polling again.
   sleep 5
done
```

When one or more queries finish, the process calls more shell scripts (bench${Q_num}.sh below) to initiate more queries or sessions. The trick is to call this shell in background mode, indicated by the "&". There may be small gaps where the concurrency is not at the proper level, but that represents a small amount of time when the process is sleeping.

Benchmark Reporting

A lot of truly important features of this program have been omitted. A comprehensive benchmark program captures and logs DDL, explain plans, Join Index information, and statistics for all tables and views involved.

This information comes in very handy when problems arise and there is a need to compare old results to current results. It may very well be that the prior benchmark that was run several months earlier had a few more statistics collected than the most recent execution. Without capturing this information, no one would ever know.

It all depends on how far someone wants to take it, but this program can be smart enough to rebuild Join Indices if missing, collect missing statistics, revoke and grant back logons to users, and the list goes on. At a minimum, the program should backup or rename the BENCH_STATS table, so this information can be easily retrieved far into the future and results can be easily compared.

Tip - A comprehensive benchmark program captures and logs DDL, explain plans, Join Index information, and statistics for all tables and views involved.

Benchmark Reporting Macro

The following macro should be run at the end of the benchmark process and really should be incorporated in the automation above so that it gets logged and documented with the rest of the job. This macro generates the reports that get communicated to management and other concerned parties. Following the macro example produces one such report.

```
REPLACE MACRO CSQL_MACRO.BENCH_RPT
As ( -- Reports on Start, End and Duration of the entire benchmark.
SELECT
MIN(Q_BEGIN_TS) AS START_TIME,
MAX(Q_END_TS) AS END_TIME,
MAX(Q_END_TS) - MIN(Q_BEGIN_TS) HOUR(4) TO SECOND(0) AS
BENCHMARK_DURATION
FROM CSQL_CLASS.BENCH_STATS;

-- Reports on Percent done per hour.
SELECT END_HOUR "END_HOUR",RUN_CNT "RUN CNT",
CSUM(RUN_CNT,END_HOUR)/4.00 "PERCENT DONE"
FROM (SELECT  (Q_END_TS - A.MIN_TIME HOUR) END_HOUR,
          COUNT(*) RUN_CNT
          FROM CSQL_CLASS.BENCH_STATS,
               (SELECT   MIN(Q_BEGIN_TS)  AS MIN_TIME
                FROM CSQL_CLASS.BENCH_STATS) A
GROUP BY 1) B  ORDER BY 1;

-- Reports on the MIN and MAX rows returned for each Query
SELECT Q_NUM "QUERY NUM",
MIN(Q_ROWS) "MIN ROWS",
MAX(Q_ROWS) "MAX ROWS"
FROM CSQL_CLASS.BENCH_STATS
GROUP BY 1  ORDER BY 1;
-- Reports on the AVG, MIN, and MAX run time of each Query type
SELECT Q_NUM "QUERY NUM",
AVG(Q_END_TS - Q_BEGIN_TS HOUR(4) TO SECOND(0)) "AVG TIME",
MIN(Q_END_TS - Q_BEGIN_TS HOUR(4) TO SECOND(0)) "MIN TIME",
MAX(Q_END_TS - Q_BEGIN_TS HOUR(4) TO SECOND(0)) "MAX TIME",
COUNT(*) "TIMES RUN"
FROM CSQL_CLASS.BENCH_STATS
GROUP BY 1 ORDER BY 3 DESC; );
```

Report Example

QUERY NUM	*AVG TIME*	*MIN TIME*	*MAX TIME*	*TIMES RUN*
12	1:41:09	1:25:17	1:48:49	4
26	1:24:57	1:05:16	1:37:53	20
17	1:11:02	1:04:50	1:16:54	4
14	0:53:57	0:36:20	1:01:54	4
22	0:29:16	0:23:36	0:35:28	8
24	0:18:13	0:17:45	0:18:38	4
6	0:18:33	0:14:43	0:24:43	24

This report lists the average, minimum, and maximum run time for each query type and how many times each ran.

Summary

Benchmarks are used to measure the overall system performance before and after migrations, upgrades, patch implementations, TASM implementations, and even certain major project implementations, etc. Not every project implementation will impact the performance benchmarks or the users' workload.

At the very minimum, this process should be run just before and immediately after every major implementation, every upgrade, and every patch. It is run just before each so that there is a baseline to compare to after. It should also run on a scheduled or periodic basis as data volumes grow, new features and functionality are introduced, hardware ages, etc. Review the reports closely to make sure all queries run successfully, timely, and produce the correct results.

Here is the last piece of advice on this topic. Don't react too quickly to unexpected benchmark results until the proper diagnosis has been conducted to rule out internal oversights.

Shell Script Extract Example

```
Main_Proc()
{

print $(date) '  -  STARTING Canary Query!!!!.......'    >>${HISTFI}
# Call to this shell script is in background mode . important!
${HOMEDIR}/canary01.sh ${T_LOG} > ${OUTFI}  &
sleep 5

#  Have to check status every 5 seconds and email and page.
while [$(grep "*** Logon successfully completed." ${OUTFI} |wc -l) -lt 1]
  do
    if [ sleep_cnt -eq 6 ]
    then
       problem_found='CANARY logon is taking too long '
       MAIL_DBA
    elif [ sleep_cnt -ge 12 ]
    then
       problem_found='CANARY logon is taking FAR too long '
       PAGE_DBA
    fi

    print $(date) ' -   Sleeping 5 seconds for Login...'    >>${HISTFI}
    sleep 5
    sleep_cnt=sleep_cnt+1
  done

sleep_cnt=0
```

<Continued Next Page>

<Continued>

```
# Have to check status every 10 seconds.
while [$(grep "*** Exiting BTEQ..." ${OUTFI} |wc -l) -lt 1]
  do
    if [ sleep_cnt -eq 9 ]
    then
      problem_found='CANARY running long'
      MAIL_DBA
    elif [ sleep_cnt -ge 25 ]
    then
      problem_found='CANARY running FAR too long'
      PAGE_DBA
    fi

    print $(date) ' - Sleep 10 seconds for Canary...' >>${HISTFI}
    sleep 10
    sleep_cnt=sleep_cnt+1

  done

print $(date) ' - ENDING Canary Query!!!!...' >>${HISTFI}
}
```

There are many factors that can affect a query's response, such as network issues, missing or stale statistics on tables or Join Indices, a down AMP or node, other missing indices, and much more. Get to know this query intimately so that you can respond immediately when something goes amiss. If logons start paging, don't waste any time. This indicates you may have a serious problem, and you don't want users and management calling you before the cause has been determined. This canary process should help you be proactive and resolve problems before they are widespread.

The final word to this story is reporting and trending. Canaries should be analyzed daily and trended over time to determine possible peaks and valleys in performance. If spikes in canary response time are observed in a given day, there might be a workload issue of user query that may need to be addressed. A trending analysis needs to be conducted on the performance of these queries to determine how the system is truly performing over time. Incorporating Canary trending reports in conjunction with benchmarks and DBQL analysis will help determine if upgrade time is approaching.

Unfinished Canary SQL Example

Here are a few basic queries for analysis. First, identify canary queries that never finished during the current month.

```
SELECT  *
FROM  CANARY_STATS
WHERE COMPLETION_IND <> 'Y' AND
WHERE Q_BEGIN_TS (DATE ) BETWEEN
        (DATE - (DATE MOD 100) +1) AND DATE
ORDER BY Q_BEGIN_TS DESC;
```

The query above will hopefully return no rows, but if it does, then investigation is needed. Either the canary query was running at the time of this execution or for some reason the query was aborted between the time it was logged and the time it was supposed to finish.

Canary Reporting SQL Example

```
SELECT C.*,
   CAST( CAST (C.Q_BEGIN_TS AS FORMAT 'YYYY-MM')
           AS CHAR(7) ) AS YEAR_MONTH,
   EXTRACT(HOUR FROM C.Q_BEGIN_TS) AS HOUR_DAY,
   C.Q_END_TS - C.Q_BEGIN_TS
   HOUR(4) TO SECOND(0) AS ELAPSED_TM,
   EXTRACT (HOUR FROM ELAPSED_TM)*3600 +
   EXTRACT(MINUTE FROM ELAPSED_TM)*60 +
   EXTRACT(SECOND FROM ELAPSED_TM) AS SECONDS,
   CASE WHEN HOUR_DAY BETWEEN 8 AND 17
           THEN 'Y'
           ELSE 'N'
   END AS OFF_HOUR,
   CASE WHEN SC.DAY_OF_WEEK IN (1,7)
           THEN 'Y'
           ELSE 'N'
   END AS WEEK_END
FROM CANARY_STATS  C
JOIN SYS_CALENDAR.CALENDAR SC
ON C.Q_BEGIN_TS (DATE) = SC.CALENDAR_DATE
WHERE C.Q_BEGIN_TS (DATE ) BETWEEN
           (DATE - (DATE MOD 100) +1) AND DATE
ORDER BY C.Q_BEGIN_TS DESC;
```

The query above calculates the elapsed time, hour of day, weekend, number of seconds and more for the current month. This query will help you report nicely on business hour activity, and let you graphically display meaningful reports. Consider incorporating this into a view and even joining this information to a company holiday table to get even more useful information.

Make sure to identify any queries that fall outside the expected SLA and investigate. DBQL tables and reports will give a better picture of what was happening during problematic response times. From the information provided from the query above, reports and counts can be generated by hour of day, business hours, and by categorizing the response time into buckets of less than five seconds, less than ten seconds, greater than thirty seconds, etc. SLA expectations can be set according to these buckets.

We have just illustrated one possible approach to a canary query implementation. Make sure the canary query runs in at least one of the same resource partitions as the rest of the user community. This canary query should represent a typical business transaction, and should run at frequent and defined periods throughout the day.

Remember, monitoring and reporting on response time only shows half the picture. Just as important, logon times need monitoring as well and then send out alerts when excessive times are encountered. It is a bit harder to report on logon times. Once the infrastructure is built to execute the canary and capture the information, then results need to be reported. Look for times when the queries never finished and when there were spikes in elapsed time.

Over time, averages and baselines for these queries will be established so that elapsed times can be compared to SLAs. These are data points in a complete analysis of system performance. This information can be used to extrapolate future execution and performance metrics as well.

It's a good time to mention that TASM may throw a small wrench into this process. TASM may change the rules for analyzing these queries, depending on the complexity of the TASM rules that are set. Canary queries might start falling into different response time buckets after changing the rules.

This does not mean that user performance is adversely affected, but changes may be needed in the canary reporting process. Canary queries may actually take longer, but the overall workload for users may actually be improved. There is no exact science here, but we did want to shed awareness that TASM may change the game a little.

Just make sure not to tune TASM, Priority Scheduler or any other workload management tool so that canary queries are given higher priority to perform better. They need to be representative of normal business activity and stay that way.

Summary

Every database platform should set up a Canary Query process to both monitor daily performance as well as trend performance over time. It provides a true picture of what the users see in terms of performance. Teradata provides heartbeat queries as part of Teradata Manager and Viewpoint applications. In this chapter, we described an alternative approach that provides a few additional benefits and some more flexibility.

We defined a Canary Query as a well established and static query that gets executed in the database on a frequent and set interval. If the query does not return or takes too long, then someone should be notified. The method described in this chapter also alerts if the logon for the session takes too long. This is actually the most informative measure of when something is amiss on the system and why we advocate this approach.

Finally, these Canary queries should be run in the same manner as the users they are trying to imitate. Most likely, you will set up at least one canary query to see how the everyday user is performing. However, another idea may be to run multiple canary queries against different resource partitions. Whatever approach you take, keep the process as simple and easy to maintain as possible. Please try to avoid using too many resources to monitor and report on canary performance. Letting canary processes put unnecessary stress on the system would be counterproductive.

Chapter 13 - Security Techniques

Grants
Roles
Column Masking
Profiles

The primary purpose of this chapter is to provide alternatives for securing data and discuss benefits and costs of different approaches. Whatever approach is chosen, it should be efficient and flexible along with meeting the security requirements as well. Make sure to pick a solution that is not only efficient for the administrators and architects, but is also straight-forward and efficient for the users as well. This chapter does not discuss database or logon authentication.

We will discuss grants, roles, views, column level masking, and a new technique of using profiles to perform column level masking. The profile solution mentioned in this chapter is especially worth paying attention to and understanding. Sophisticated Teradata users may even want to flip directly to that solution.

It is likely that none of these solutions will meet your needs, but the point of this chapter is to spawn ideas and get the thinking process going.

There is a good chance that you will come up with your own security design or choose a hybrid approach from the following. This chapter does not address user creation, authentication and password maintenance. Let's start off with the basics first.

Grants

The simplest solution is to provide access at the database or object level through the GRANT command. If this solution suffices for your design and requirements, then this is the absolute best way to go. Grants can be issued with the allness option so that new users and databases inherit the same grants. This greatly reduces the maintenance burden. By all means, if you can get by with granting access at the database level to all users of a given hierarchy, then please go for it and flip to the next chapter.

Chances are that this will not suffice alone, and that you will need to incorporate an additional approach as well. This discussion will not touch on all aspects of GRANT and REVOKE statements, such as monitor privileges, roles, functions, types, syntax, etc. We will focus on database-level grants and common obstacles and solutions.

To GRANT Select on a database to everyone in a given hierarchy, just perform the following:

```
GRANT SEL ON CSQL_VIEWS TO ALL USER_DBS;
```

The command above will grant select on the view database to all databases and users under the USER_DBS hierarchy. All new databases and users created under USER_DBS will inherit the same access right.

Grants can be issued at the object level, database, or user level. Access rights granted at the database level take precedence over object level grants. For example, if you grant select on a database to a user, then revoking select on one of the objects in that same database from the user will have no effect. The database-level grant will take precedence and the user will still be able to access the object. The following example illustrates this scenario.

As Administrator or database owner:

```
GRANT SEL ON CSQL_VIEWS TO TESTUSER;

REVOKE SEL ON CSQL_VIEWS.JOB_V FROM TESTUSER;
```

As TESTUSER user:

```
SEL COUNT(*) FROM  CSQL_VIEWS.JOB_V;


Count(*)
5
```

The example above shows that revoking individual access rights when the same rights are granted at the database level has no effect. There often seems to be confusion with access rights when trying to get views and stored procedures to work. The rule is fairly simple.

The database where the view resides needs to have the necessary access to the object or database WITH GRANT OPTION appended to the end of the GRANT statement. Take note that as long as you have CREATE VIEW authority, you will be able to create the view, but if the database where you are creating the view does not have WITH GRANT OPTION on the target database or databases, then the view will not work.

Without this important clause, you will receive the dreaded error "3523: An owner referenced by user does not have SELECT WITH GRANT OPTION access to ...". The same grant is needed for stored procedures that access other databases or objects as well.

For example, in order to create views that work, the view database needs to have SELECT...WITH GRANT OPTION granted on the target table or view database as such:

```
GRANT SELECT ON  CSQL_CLASS
TO CSQL_VIEWS  WITH GRANT OPTION;
```

Roles

Roles are a collection of access rights that are assigned to a name for a given work function. Roles have their purpose, but it is important to know their limitations, and that they do require considerable maintenance as compared to database-level grants. Roles cannot be granted to users or databases with allness. Therefore, every time a new user is created that needs the specific role, it must be granted individually.

Roles can be incorporated in stored procedures or macros, but the important thing to take away is that the role grants will not be inherited. Roles need to be maintained at the individual user level. It is important to realize that grants on objects to roles will be lost if those objects are dropped and recreated.

With each occurrence, the grants to the role need to be reissued. This is not true for database level grants, whose grants are retained. If a view is replaced, then the grants are retained even for roles. This assumes the use of a good design that enforces users to access tables via views with appropriate levels of access locking. Therefore, replacing the individual views will not be an issue.

Tip - It is important to realize that grants on objects to roles will be lost if those objects are dropped and recreated. With each occurrence, the grants to the role need to be reissued.

Make the decision to use roles based on your requirements, and use roles only when necessary. If granting at the database level will suffice, then do that. Don't create a role and then grant access to a single database to that role. This is a waste and can be accomplished with a single database grant. Roles are useful when granting access on a set of specific objects or databases to a given job function. Roles are particularly useful when sets of tables within a specific database need to be assigned to different job functions. Roles will also help minimize the number of rights in the AccessRights table. This has always been a selling point for roles.

Proliferation of Grants Example

As depicted in the following overly simplified picture, there are three users, three views, and nine grants.

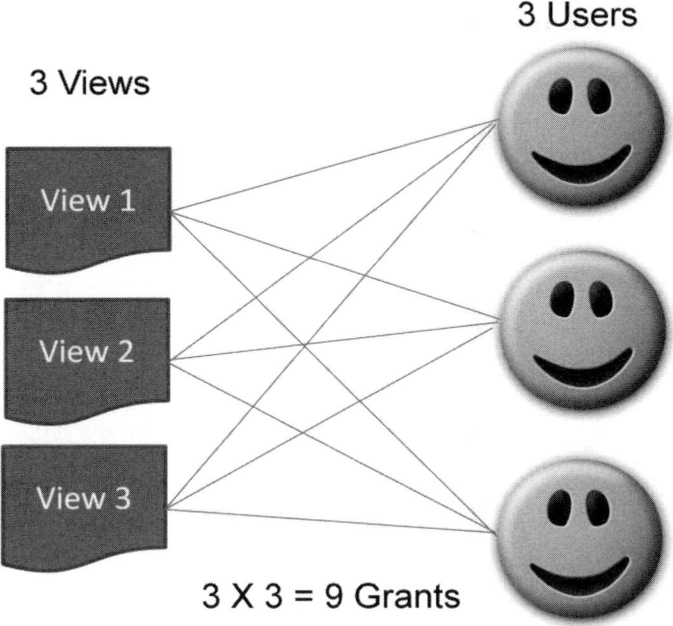

As views are added, access to the new views has to be granted to each user. The same is true for new users. The illustration is uncomplicated and obviously easy to maintain with simple grant commands at this point. Now imagine 500 views, and 100 users. The number of grants required is 500*100 or 50,000 grants. With a single role, each view can be assigned to the role with 500 grants, and then the role can be assigned to each user with 100 more grants for a total of 600 grants instead.

Adding another view or role is a single grant statement for each new view at this point. This example assumes that there are other views or objects in the same database that will be assigned to a different group or set of users. If not, then access can be granted at the database level to each user or with one command to every user under a designated hierarchy. The nice thing about this is that any new users will inherit the same grants. Role security requires the need to continuously grant every necessary role to any new users.

Views

We refer to views and not tables in most examples because it's a best practice not to allow users direct access to tables without at least one level of views with access locking on the table. As mentioned in subsequent sections, this will help avoid locking scenarios with load procedures. In addition to providing a degree of program logic, views also provide a layer of security by selecting only required columns, masking columns, encrypting columns, case logic, etc. These techniques are discussed in further detail below.

A certain degree of security can be achieved by creating views for each business purpose or job role. These views can reside in the same database and be granted access through roles, or they can reside in different databases and access granted at the database level, roles, or both. Either way, this will likely lead to a maintenance or administrative nightmare, requiring a proliferation of views, databases, roles, or all of the above. The following solutions or alternatives are more flexible, and avoid the need for such proliferations.

Table-driven Column Masking

There are different methods for masking columns, but some are more efficient than others. The rest of this chapter is devoted to a certain form of row-level security and a few ways to achieve it. There are certainly more ways to attack this problem, but hopefully, some insight can be gained through these alternatives.

The goal is to make the process as efficient and flexible as possible. This method involves implementing a control table to house each user's security access combinations, and a row-level indicator on the target table to mark each row as a given security type. The views will then cross-join the target tables to a single row of the user control table where the current userid equals the userid stored in the control table.

This does perform a Cartesian join between a single row of the control table and the entire target table. The product join (where "1=1") in the following explain plan example illustrates this Cartesian product:

Explain Output

```
Spool 2 and CSQL_CLASS.CUST_TAB are joined using a product join, with a join
condition of ("(1=1)"). The result goes into Spool 1 (group_amps),...
```

Full table scans can take a hit in performance, but the ease and flexibility of the solution may be worth it. It is imperative that to design an infrastructure for maintaining this user control table. Make sure that all user access is stored and maintained correctly.

Example of User Security Control Table

Stored procedures are integral to this process. The stored procedures will insert into this control table when new users are created or restored. It will update the control table when security access is changed, and will delete from the control table when users are dropped. This can be handled outside of stored procedures, but not as efficiently.

```
CREATE SET TABLE CSQL_CLASS.USR_SEC ,
   FALLBACK ,
   NO BEFORE JOURNAL,
   NO AFTER JOURNAL,
   CHECKSUM = DEFAULT
   (
    USR_ID  VARCHAR(30) NOT NULL,
    EMP_SEC_CD CHAR(1),
    MGR_SEC_CD CHAR(1),
    AUD_SEC_CD CHAR(1))
UNIQUE PRIMARY INDEX USR_SEC_UP ( USR_ID );

INS CSQL_CLASS.USR_SEC ('JOKER', 'E', '','');
INS CSQL_CLASS.USR_SEC ('BATMAN', 'E', 'M','');
INS CSQL_CLASS.USR_SEC ('SYSADM', '', '','A');
```

The above example illustrates one method for masking columns depending on a row-level identifier. Base views are listed as well to demonstrate best practices for access locking.

This should be a relatively small table containing a single row for each application or database user. It includes a column for the user identifier, a secure code for employee records, manager records, and a code for auditor only records. These security codes determine a given user's level of security. Create a base view to guarantee access locks during select access.

Base View with Access Locking

```
REPLACE VIEW CSQL_VIEWS.USR_SEC (
USR_ID,
EMP_SEC_CD,
MGR_SEC_CD,
AUD_SEC_CD
) AS LOCKING CSQL_CLASS.USR_SEC
FOR ACCESS SELECT
USR_ID,
EMP_SEC_CD,
MGR_SEC_CD,
AUD_SEC_CD
FROM CSQL_CLASS.USR_SEC;
```

Customer Table with row-level security code

```
CREATE SET TABLE CSQL_CLASS.CUST_TAB ,
   NO FALLBACK ,
   NO BEFORE JOURNAL,
   NO AFTER JOURNAL,
   CHECKSUM = DEFAULT
   (
    CUST_NBR INTEGER,
    CUST_NM VARCHAR(20),
    PHONE_NBR CHAR(8),
    SEC_CD CHAR(1))
UNIQUE PRIMARY INDEX ( CUST_NBR )
INDEX ( CUST_NM )
INDEX ( PHONE_NBR );
```

The example above shows a table with a security code (SEC_CD), which will be used in subsequent views to identify a row type for the customer data. This code will be used later to determine if the PHONE_NBR column should be masked or not. Possible values for this SEC_CD will be "E" for Employee, "M" for Manager, and "A" for Auditor rows.

Base View on Customer table with Access Locking

```
REPLACE VIEW CSQL_VIEWS.CUST_TAB (
CUST_NBR,
CUST_NM,
PHONE_NBR,
SEC_CD
) AS LOCKING CSQL_CLASS.CUST_TAB FOR ACCESS
SELECT
CUST_NBR,
CUST_NM,
PHONE_NBR,
SEC_CD
FROM CSQL_CLASS.CUST_TAB;
```

Example of Masked or Secured View

```
REPLACE VIEW CSQL_VIEWS.CUST_TAB_SEC AS
SELECT
    C.CUST_NBR,
    C.CUST_NM,
    CASE WHEN C.SEC_CD = U.EMP_SEC_CD
           THEN C.PHONE_NBR
           WHEN C.SEC_CD = U.MGR_SEC_CD
           THEN C.PHONE_NBR
           WHEN C.SEC_CD = U.AUD_SEC_CD
           THEN C.PHONE_NBR
           ELSE '***********'
    END PHONE_NBR
FROM CSQL_VIEWS.CUST_TAB C
CROSS JOIN CSQL_VIEWS.USR_SEC U
WHERE U.USR_ID=USER;
```

The example above is not a static view, which shows the same data to every user the same way. Instead, depending on who is accessing it, the result may change from one user to another. The view definition shown above is coded in such a way that the Phone Number information is masked for those users who are not authorized to see it and presented in clear text for those who are authorized.

To that effect, a CASE statement is used to check if the value of the SEC_CD column matches any one of the three security access codes in the USR_SEC table. Further down in the view definition, one can see the cross join of the two tables with only one record of the USR_SEC table as limited by the "WHERE U.USR_ID=USER;" clause, which filters out all but the active user.

The SEC_CD in each row of the CUST_TAB table will determine if the user can see the masked column. This example assumes that only the PHONE_NBR contains sensitive data and is in need of masking.

If the SEC_CD for the row does not match the access in the USR_SEC table, then asterisks will be displayed for the PHONE_NBR. Other customer related data may need to be secured or masked as well, such as credit card numbers, social security numbers, addresses, etc.

Performance is impacted in this solution by the CROSS JOIN, and occasionally the optimizer could make suboptimal decisions. SQL will not work the same for all users, which may cause skewing or other issues. For example, one user may have full access and no columns are masked. They may share this same SQL with another user with limited access. This user may get masked columns returned, and the SQL may not return anything, get skewed results, fail, or be meaningless. This is really a training issue.

There are definitely other ways to accomplish this, but this should be enough to start the ball rolling or spawn ideas.

Profile-driven Column Masking

The following alternative is very similar to the prior solution, but uses PROFILES to drive the security for each user. The benefit of this solution is found in performance. There is almost no overhead to this solution, and no Cartesian join between tables. Actually, there is no join at all. There is no need for a control table, but we suggest

Chapter 15 - Software Upgrades

Project
Management
Planning
Communication
Testing

This chapter is focused primarily on major *Software Upgrades*. Much of this information and more can be found in a document produced by the Teradata Service Focus Team that the author of this book coauthored and provided the initial template. However, many of the steps necessary to perform major hardware upgrades and minor software upgrades may also apply.

Upgrading from Teradata version 5.1 to 6.0 is an example of a major upgrade. If the first number in the version changes, this indicates that it's a major upgrade, but sometimes changing the second number may constitute a major upgrade. An example of this is when upgrading from Teradata 6.0 to Teradata 6.2. There are enough changes in the software and architecture, that this would require treating this like a major release and a major upgrade.

Any successful software upgrade involves careful organization, planning, communication, implementation, and testing that starts long before the actual implementation date.

Teradata maintains control over software quality and the procedures for installations. Although it's not possible to control every aspect of the Teradata upgrade, it is possible to control the procedures that are necessary from a Teradata customer perspective. Mistakes in any of these efforts cannot be afforded, but we will focus only on what we can control in order to make the upgrade process as seamless as possible.

Project Management

First, realize that upgrading Teradata is no trivial matter. It is a very complicated, resource intensive and costly venture that needs to be treated as a corporate or official project. Management buy-in is necessary and resources need to be assigned for project management, DBA, testing, development, client software assistance, operations, etc.

Effective communication, scheduling, accountability, and coordination are imperative for an effort of this magnitude. Therefore, a dedicated project manager of some sort is needed, whether they are certified in project management or not. Planning and status meetings should include these various resources, and should include the Teradata Customer Service Representative (CSR) as well.

Don't throw away those old project plans ever! Revisit them after each project completes to capture any missing tasks or circumstances. This chapter is a product of many project plans over numerous years. This plan will be used again and again to make sure all bases are covered during every upgrade. It could be embarrassing if a step is missed that was also missed on a prior effort, so maintain this document for recollection.

Upgrade Planning

Take time to get educated first on new software version features and any complexities surrounding the upgrade process. Create a presentation to educate others on new features in layman's terms, or pilfer a Partners presentation and present it to those people that are interested or who will help sell the idea to management.

The initiation of the upgrade process should result from a feature rich new version and not just because a maintenance period is up. People need to get excited about the newer technology and the more people that are talking about it the better.

Here are some sources for identifying version capabilities:

- Partners presentations.
- Class and certification material often identify new features.
- Version manuals provide Release definitions and Release Summaries - downloadable from the Teradata website at http://www.info.teradata.com.
- Reserved Words Document - helps identify new reserved words that might necessitate changes to the physical structures or SQL. Scripts can be

developed to validate database objects for reserved words or use the scripts that Teradata provides. It's a good idea to search stored procedures and DBQL data for reserved word usage as well. We suggest staying ahead of this one by including these checks in day-to-day DDL validation steps.

- The Package Comparison Tool located on the Teradata@YourService website - by displaying the DR's (Discrepancy Reports) in each version, better decisions can be made on risk and reward.

Communication

Use these documents to inform and educate users. This information can be posted to a corporate website or share point site. More effectively, try holding classes or lunch and learn sessions.

Inform users how to change their own DDL and SQL to eliminate reserved words. This is also an excellent time for them to drop obsolete objects that they own or have created. Reaffirm and inform users that all of their objects and data will be backed up prior to their clean-up effort and the upgrade.

The next step in the upgrade process is to identify and inventory all the Teradata client and utility dependent applications in the environment. Consider all applications such as homegrown programs or DBA scripts, Business Intelligence software, ETL tools, Teradata Manager, SAS, Backup and Recovery software such as Netvault and Netbackup, and the standard Teradata Tools and Utilities.

Determine if the new Teradata version will require third-party applications using Teradata to be upgraded first or not. Just because a third-party tool claims to be certified and compatible does not prevent the need for thorough testing.

A thorough test plan absolutely needs to be

> *Tip* - Not only should you continually make sure that your databases, objects, and column names don't contain reserved words, but you should try to avoid words that have the potential of becoming a reserved word in the future. Following a set naming convention and using abbreviations will help in this regard.

conducted that includes all functionality that is currently used and maybe even new functionality that has potential for use.

Don't underestimate the work needed to correct reserved word violations. It may be harder to find reserved words in user SQL, but it's easier to fix. Database names, Table names and column names that are reserved words can be very time consuming and arduous to change. It all depends on how engrained these are in the application and ETL.

Something as simple as a database name becoming a reserved word can delay an upgrade by months while this hard-coded value is modified in hundreds or thousands of ETL jobs, user queries, BI reports, views, macros, stored procedures, and DBA maintenance jobs.

Develop a benchmark test that will be run at least once prior to the upgrade and at least once after the upgrade. This benchmark needs to be repeatable, consistent, and long enough to measure results. Benchmark testing needs to be a standard ingredient in every test plan. Without such a test, it is virtually impossible to measure the Return on Investment (ROI) for any upgrade.

Capture true workload queries from DBQL that represent a range of tactical, canary, short-running, long-running, simple and complex queries and run them in exactly the same order and with the same concurrency every time. Teradata is amazing in its ability to provide consistent times on benchmark tests. Be intimately knowledgeable of the queries and the objects involved in the benchmark.

There are many factors that influence the performance of queries, so be sure to have the proper statistics collected, indexes and Join Indexes built, etc. for each benchmark test. Most importantly, make sure the benchmarks are run on a quiescent system (period of low or no activity).

Capture Explain output, statistics and elapsed times for each query on each benchmark execution. If a benchmark produces alarming results, then compare the explain plans to see what changed. For example, this could illustrate that a Join Index is no longer used because of missing statistics, Join Index is missing, or the optimizer chose not to use it anymore. The latter case is worrisome, but the other two issues would require collecting stats, rebuilding the Join Index and rerunning the benchmark test. For further information, please refer to the Performance Benchmarking chapter for further information.

Regression Testing

Regression testing is needed in addition to benchmark testing. We assume that an adequate test system is available, but most Teradata customers use their development systems to install the new version and regression test. The only downfall to this is that environments will be out of synch for the duration of the testing process, which could very well be a considerable amount of time.

The benchmark queries mentioned above will be a great place to start testing. It is a good idea test a full load schedule, conduct any patch tests that may be set up, and test every application that accesses Teradata. It is a great idea to test utilities that are used as well, such as Fastexport, FastLoad, Mulitload, TPump, TPT, and ARC.

A copy of production data would make the best test bed, but a subset of this data would suffice if TSET is used to copy the statistics and demographics to the test system. Run the benchmarks, user queries, loads, BI interfaces, and compare the explain plans and response times.

If the response times for any queries are abnormally high, then they need to be run again on a quiescent system. If they are still high, make all the necessary statistics are collected on the tables and Join Indexes. It could be as simple as missing an index or Join Index. We suggest automating a validation script that can be run before and immediately after the upgrade. This may save a lot of time.

It is not uncommon for a small number of queries to run longer than they did prior to the upgrade. This can be due to optimizer changes, but a large number of longer running queries are obviously undesirable and worrisome. Hopefully, most queries run much faster or the same, resulting in faster overall run times.

> *Tip* – Be sure to uninstall old client software prior to installing new software. It's a common issue to have DLLs and registry entries left behind that adversely affect new installs.

Before upgrading the Teradata-supplied Tools and Utilities (TTU) software, make sure all third-party software is already upgraded or certified on the target release of the Teradata software. Assuming that an inventory was taken of all the TTU applications, servers, workstations, etc., it is time to start upgrading all Teradata client software.

Basically, make sure this TTU version will work with the database version, OS version and any third-party tools. The TTU may be installed on UNIX, Windows, Linux, etc. and is comprised of the Teradata ODBC driver, BTEQ, Index and Statistics Wizards, Query Scheduler, SQL Assistant, Teradata Administrator (WinDDI) and more.

Upgrading the third-party software and TTU should be treated as a mini project and should have its own implementation plan. Keep an eye on patches and releases. It's possible for new patch releases to come out while the implementation is being planned.

It's time to get developers, DBAs and users to start testing the new TTU version and third-party tools. This is where a repetitive test suite comes in handy. Perform regression tests on commonly used features and especially on any problems that occurred in the past, regardless of prior certifications. Be prepared to apply software patches as problems are found.

Backup and Recovery (BAR) software such as ARCMAIN, NetBackup and NetVault may need to be upgraded as well before upgrading the database. The Teradata roadmap will help determine database version and software compatibility, but make sure the operating system will support the new version of BAR software. Find windows to perform the BAR upgrade where no significant backups are required.

Backup the master server, catalog and all configuration files prior to the upgrade. Test and verify that older versions of media server clients still work with the new master server. Now the media servers can be upgraded and tested by running backups and restores to and from the local drives. If possible, try performing a disaster recovery test by backing up DBC and restoring on a test system to ensure that the new version of Arcmain will restore the prior version of the system.

Now it's finally time to upgrade. Hopefully by now, it should be obvious why upgrades should be considered a major project initiative. The following are checklists that should be followed at a minimum to ensure a successful upgrade.

Teradata Pre-Upgrade Checklist

This section concerns those tasks that need to be done shortly before the Teradata software is upgraded. This is a typical list of things to do:

- ☐ Double-check that all reserved words have been eliminated from the Teradata system.

- ☐ It is a good practice to reboot all nodes one week prior to the upgrade.

- ☐ Capture DBS control settings, SysSecDefaults, ResUsage, TDWM, PSF settings, TASM settings, etc. This is not just for recovering if something goes wrong, but to make sure any settings don't get dramatically altered during the upgrade. Try to eliminate as many factors from changing as possible.

Executing dbscontrol (MP-RAS - as root)

```
# /tpasw/bin/dbscontrol
> modify systemfe=true
> display
```

- ☐ If possible, make at least two full All-AMP backups of vital data, and *at least* one copy of all data. Cluster backups may require significant restore times if the AMP configuration changes and it has to restore serially. Cluster backups also require all tapes in the cluster to be successful. One bad tape and the whole backup is useless.

- ☐ Run scandisk and checktable early enough to correct any issues found. Run checktable at level 3 on DBC only and at level 2 for all other tables.

Executing scandisk (MP-RAS)

```
# /etc/gsc/bin/cnsremote scandisk
```

Executing checktable (MP-RAS)

```
# /etc/gsc/bin/cnsremote checktable check dbc at level three
with no error limit skiplocks priority=m
```

☐ Clean out leftover Spool via the "updatespace" procedure. This can be started from cnsterm.

Executing cnsterm (MP-RAS)

```
# cnsterm 6
> start updatespace

### Now go to the window updatespace started in.  View the results and quit.
   # cnsterm 1
   > quit
   > update spool space for <uid>;
   update spool space for <uid>;
   Updating space for <uid>
   Space updated for <uid>;
   Enter QUIT or CONTINUE.
   > QUIT
```

☐ Capture DDLs of Hash, Join Indexes, Triggers and UDFs. These should be dropped prior to the upgrade.

To identify Join Indexes

```
SELECT  * FROM DBC.INDICES
WHERE INDEXTYPE = 'J';
```

☐ If using journaling, then the journal tables may need to be dropped prior to the upgrade.

☐ Disable DBQL and offload it to a history repository. DBQL needs to be restarted after the upgrade is complete.

☐ Purge AmpUsage over 90 or 180 days old unless more is needed for some reason.

☐ Resolve checktable issues (tables in a pending load status). Many Utilities leave work and log tables from failed load jobs. These can be dropped if they are not current and still needed.

Teradata Upgrade

It's finally time to upgrade the Teradata server software. The software upgrade is typically performed by the Teradata site CSR. Here is a checklist of activities that the customer DBA may perform:

- ☐ Make sure at least one full successful backup is available and valid. We suggest multiple backups if possible.
- ☐ Log off and lock out all unnecessary users by revoking logons, and abort remaining user sessions if there are any.
- ☐ Shutdown the Viewpoint, TASM and/or Teradata Manager servers and associated services.
- ☐ Shutdown any other applications or third-party applications such as Visual Edge, AQM, Query Scheduler, etc.
- ☐ Stop any job schedulers such as cron, Control M, etc.
- ☐ Take a last minute backup of DBC.
- ☐ Shutdown backup applications and schedulers such as NetVault and NetBackup.
- ☐ Run checktable "pendingop" and clean up any unresolved issues or tables in load ready state:

Executing checktable (MP-RAS) - All Tables

```
/etc/gsc/bin/cnsremote checktable check all tables at level pendingop
```

- ☐ Ensure that all Join Indexes, Hash Indexes, Triggers and UDFs have been dropped. Then rebuild and recreate these after the upgrade.
- ☐ Change the password for DBC just prior as well. This password will need to be given to the CSR and changed back after the upgrade.
- ☐ Notify the Teradata CSR to start the upgrade process.

Post-Upgrade Steps

After the CSR has completed and validated his piece of the upgrade, he will need to notify the DBA so the following steps can be completed:

- ☐ Change the password for DBC back or to a new password that CSR does not know.

- ☐ Run checktable DBC only at level 3. This should only take a few minutes.

Executing checktable (MP-RAS)

```
# /etc/gsc/bin/cnsremote checktable check dbc at level
three with no error limit skiplocks priority=m
```

- ☐ Run scandisk and checktable again to verify the rest of the file system is clean.

- ☐ Create another backup of DBC and any other critical databases. If any new system databases were created as part of the upgrade, remember to grant the appropriate dump/restore privileges on them and add them to the BAR scripts. This will be a good test for backups, but some restores need to be tested as well.

- ☐ Enable DBQL, Access logging, System Security, Priority scheduler, etc. as before.

- ☐ Check the DBC.SysSecDefaults table to make sure that prior settings are still being enforced.

- ☐ Restart the Viewpoint, TASM and/or Teradata Manager servers and services.

- ☐ Check/reset TDWM, DBScontrol, XCTL and PSF settings.

- ☐ Recreate Hash, Join Indexes, Triggers and UDFs that were dropped prior to the upgrade.

- ☐ Recreate journal tables (if any).

- ☐ Make sure the default date format is set correctly. This often gets changed inadvertently during patches and upgrades.

- ☐ The upgrade scripts would have identified and recompiled any Teradata Stored Procedures (TDSP).
- ☐ Recompile and test all load, DBA and user stored procedures.
- ☐ Restore DDL for system databases that may have been modified (i.e. Sys_Calendar.CALENDAR).
- ☐ Validate that statistics are collected correctly on DBC and user tables. Recollect statistics on application tables if they are recommended for this upgraded version.
- ☐ May need to adjust user spool settings if number of amps changed for some reason. With additional AMPs, then there is less space available per AMP. This could result in out of spool conditions on skewed queries.
- ☐ DBA regression testing. Run test program to validate all settings, connectivity, programs, DBC tables, procedures, etc.
- ☐ Test applications such as SQL Assistant, BTEQ, BTEQWin, OLELoad, Teradata Administrator, TASM, AQM, Teradata Manager, Viewpoint, backup and restore, etc.
- ☐ Start/confirm TDP's and enable logons.
- ☐ Restart job schedulers such as Control M, cron, Teradata Query Scheduler, etc.
- ☐ Consider running post-upgrade benchmarks and compare them to any pre-upgrade benchmarks while the system is still quiescent. Examine and publish results.
- ☐ Notify customers of system availability.
- ☐ Sign off on user acceptance of upgrade with Teradata.
- ☐ Close any change controls.

It's now time to monitor the system, document any findings from the upgrade, and conduct a lessons learned session. The information gathered at this time will be invaluable at the start of the next upgrade.

Here is an example of a lesson learned when upgrading to Linux from MP-RAS:

If upgrading to Linux, it is possible that *partitioned* tables will not be accessible without revalidating the Primary Indexes. Therefore, for every *partitioned* table, run the following:

```
ALTER TABLE Tbl_Nm  REVALIDATE PRIMARY INDEX;
```

It's celebration time!

Summary

Upgrading Teradata is no simple task, and anyone who tries to say differently needs to read what is detailed above. Any successful software upgrade involves careful organization, planning, communication, implementation, and testing that starts long before the actual implementation date. Although it's not possible to control every aspect of the Teradata upgrade, it is possible to control the procedures that are necessary from a Teradata customer perspective.

This chapter is nothing more than a compilation of lessons learned over numerous Teradata upgrades. This chapter should also serve as a checklist for the minimum tasks needed to perform a successful Teradata software upgrade. Some of these lessons and required tasks were learned the hard way, so we hope the reader benefits from us sharing this information.

Appendix A - Development DBA Service Catalog

Purpose

The purpose of this document is to capture or list all of the development DBA-related actions or involvements for new projects by phase. This is helpful when establishing tasks for new project plans and timelines.

Inception Phase

- Participate with architects to determine platform that the new database should reside on
- Participate in assessing or identifying any risks associated with the new project
- Participate in any brainstorming activities or meetings

Definition Phase

- Stay abreast of any project related documentation
- Review the logical data model
- Work with project manager in identifying and agreeing on DBA tasks needed for each project and provide estimates for all assigned tasks
- Work with the architect on developing the first draft of the physical design. Make sure Architect is aware of DBA standards, database naming conventions, reserved words and data types. Depending on the organization, the DBA may be responsible for the entire model or design.
- Ensure standards are in place for Object Naming Conventions, Reserved Word usage, Dictionary of Abbreviations and Terms, etc.
- Analyze model, data types, naming conventions, indexing, etc.

- Along with the architect and developers, design tables necessary for ETL processing and/or auditing (i.e. intermediate work tables)
- Identify any security issues, risks, resolutions, etc.
- Assist the Development team in choosing the best load strategies
- Compile a Capacity Plan - Evaluate current and future space requirements (Dev, QA, UAT, Prod)
- Assist the Project Manager by providing necessary information when needed and requesting additional system resources when needed
- Participate in all project meetings to provide status updates, provide any revised estimates and explanation of revisions and stay involved in all aspects of the project
- Participate in technical design walk-through meetings conducted by the development staff
- Create and analyze all DDL necessary for the physical data base tables, views, stored procedures, macros, etc.

Construction Phase

- Conduct or participate in the physical data model reviews
- Build or review the Backup and Recovery Plan – this may additionally entail programming the Backup Jobs/Shell Scripts, scheduling, etc.
- Participate in all project meetings to provide status updates, provide any revised estimates and explanation of revisions and stay involved in all aspects of the project
- Participate in providing solutions during walk through sessions of project specifications
- Assist in identifying and performing any needed performance benchmarks or volume stress tests. When performed, evaluate and report on the results

- Once loaded, analyze data and apply any value-based compression on tables and columns that are candidates
- Review and tune any SQL related to the project
- Identify and abide by any new policies or procedures and update any that are in need of change
- Build and validate the data models, databases, tables, views, privileges, stored procedures, and macros and make sure they get correctly promoted to the Development, QA and UAT environments

Implementation Phase

- Participate in the Production Implementation Plan (PIP) walk through sessions. Actually document the DBA PIP
- Work with developers to make sure all DBA tasks are mentioned in the Development PIP
- Participate in the Event Plan walk through sessions
- Along with Production Support, provide internal approval of Change Management tickets and implied schedule changes
- Make sure any DDL needed for production has been received from the Architect and applied back to the model
- Automate all database related activities to implement all objects, structures, grants, etc. per the event plan or Production Implementation Plan (PIP).
- Clean-up Dev, UAT, Prod environments by removing any obsolete components

Closing Phase

- As part of the project team, review and give input to the "Lessons Learned" documents
- Evaluate load and query performances and produce benchmarks if needed
- Participate in the review of the project plan and the identification of any recommended SDLC changes

Appendix B - Production DBA Service Catalog

Purpose

The purpose of this document is to capture or list all of the production Database Administration tasks or involvements as part of their job or role. This helps managers, DBAs, and customers set expectations and plan service level agreements.

The role of the Production Database Administrator is much different than the Development DBA. The major responsibility of the Production DBA is the continual maintenance and evolution of all database platforms. The DBA group is also responsible for data security, backup and recovery, and daily operations support for all enterprise database systems, not just production.

Production Services and Responsibilities

- Provide consulting services and train users and Developers on database technology, SQL tuning, load strategies, stored procedure optimization, and future version features
- Save space by analyzing column data and applying multi-value compression
- Quickly respond to and resolve database performance, access, and other database related issues
- Install and configure development, QA, UAT, and production databases
- Design and execute - benchmark testing, analysis, and communicate results of all testing
- Monitor all databases - providing details on performance bottlenecks, response times, etc.

- Complete scheduled database maintenance activities
- Refresh development, QA, and UAT environments with data from other systems when requested
- Plan and test for disaster recovery and data archiving to ensure effective protection and integrity of data assets
- Automate and implement change control, validation, and testing processes for modifications to production databases
- Enforce security standards and ensure controls are in place for end-user database access
- Provide off-hours support for the databases of critical business applications and occasionally non-production databases
- Proposing, planning, documenting, testing, and implementing Database Backup and Recovery strategies
- Work with Teradata to plan and implement software and hardware upgrades, as well as patch implementations
- Perform capacity planning and workload trending and analysis
- Work with Development DBAs to oversee and implement project initiatives
- Evaluate and make recommendations on DBA tools, BI tools, and other new technologies
- Implement efficient and secure database designs, and ensuring efficient SQL
- Establish and enforce technical standards, conventions and guidelines for database design, security, naming, configuration, backup/ recovery, disaster recovery, etc.

Appendix C - Database Naming Conventions

Purpose

This is a SAMPLE or EXAMPLE of a document to establish basic database rules, conventions or guidelines for a particular database platform. The scope of this document applies specifically to Teradata, but a similar document should be instituted to cover multiple database platforms. The true document will need to be much more thorough and comprehensive. This is meant to give ideas and act as a starting point for the real thing.

It is up to the architects and DBAs to enforce the rules since they are the gate keepers of the design and DDL. That is where tools and automation really come in handy.

Examples of Database Conventions

- Don't allow any database or object names greater than 25 characters (less the better).

  Notes on Rule: This is a rule that mainly benefits Developers and DBAs for automation and changes. However, it also provides room for suffixes and/or prefixes for index names, constraint names, etc. It's a good idea to keep names concise anyway, but it is imperative that DBAs have the ability to rename objects and append or prefix names with tags. This becomes quite difficult when the tables are already 30 characters long, and now characters have to be dropped off in order to append or prefix them to the name.

- No reserved words should be used as full names for databases, objects or columns, but they can be parts of names.

  Notes on Rule: Although more difficult, try to avoid words that have the future potential of becoming a reserved word. This may be challenging, but it's worth consideration. An easy way to avoid this is by prefixing or creating a common suffix for reserved words. Avoiding reserved words is a huge time saver when it comes upgrade time.

- Designate a certain letter that will be used later on in automation, and don't allow its use as either the first or last character. This will provide a mechanism for easy identification, so that certain objects can be included or excluded in automated processes.
- Enforce all DDL to be either UPPER or lower case, or to capitalize just the first letter of every word. Whatever it is, establish a standard and stick to it.
- Don't allow any spaces in names. Note that these are all just suggestions and examples.
- Keep all Primary Indices to a minimum number of columns without sacrificing distribution and join access. Pick a primary index that will be used in join and selection criteria, but also provides adequate distribution.
- Limit VARCHAR fields under a certain length. Then require anyone wanting to break this rule to provide a sufficient argument to do so. It is not an uncommon occurrence to see VARCHAR (2) fields even though the minimum and maximum length for the field is always 2. We have even seen data types of VARCHAR (1), which is truly a waste. The two bytes of overhead becomes a big deal as tables grow, and variable length fields are not compressible.
- Make sure Column names match data types (i.e. columns ending in "_DT" better be DATE fields only).
- For project-related and production tables, require names for indexes and constraints and establish a naming convention for each.
- Make a decision on the use of Fallback and enforce when needed.
- Use abbreviations according to the naming standards document at all times.
- Do not put any Secondary Indices on any staging

> *Tip* - Specifying the primary index in a "CREATE TABLE AS ..." statement will automatically leave off the secondary indices.

tables just because they exist on the target table. Only add indices on stage tables if it is required in subsequent load SQL. Preferably, create stage tables dynamically, and drop all secondary indices.

Special Note: Specifying the primary index in a "CREATE TABLE AS ..." statement will automatically leave off the secondary indices. A stored procedure will probably come in handy here in order to identify the correct primary index first.

- Avoid using Microsoft products (i.e. Word) to deliver or share project DDL, especially between DBAs and Architects. These applications can insert or imbed special characters that aren't visible and may negatively impact the DDL or tables structure.

- All tables will be accessed through at least one layer of base views that have Access locks on them.

- Make sure to use consistent data types across all tables for common column names or domains. For example, if working with have a column called GEND_CD and it's a CHAR(1) field, then make sure its CHAR(1) across all tables.

- Keep longer fields like VARCHAR(30) toward the end of DDL. This is due to the way Teradata stores or processes multicolumn statistics. They do it according to the order of the DDL and there is a 16 byte maximum to what is stored. This will avoid other columns being cut out of the equation.

- Try keeping all data types to fixed length and avoid VARCHAR or variable length data types where possible so multi-value compression can be applied. Remember, VARCHAR has a 2-byte overhead on every column and for every row. This is more of a consideration for voluminous tables. Two bytes is a lot when multiplied by millions or billions of rows. This is just in addition to gains that can be made through multi-value compression. The variable length columns need analysis, and this is really more pertinent to shorter-length character fields.

- When neither CHAR nor VARCHAR is clearly a superior choice, use VARCHAR because VARCHAR data requires slightly less CPU resource to manipulate than CHAR compressed data.

Note: Let the demographics of the data drive the use of VARCHAR(n) or CHAR(n) with multi-value compression. The most important factors really are Maximum field length, Average field length, and the Compressibility of the data. Compression with CHAR(n) is more efficient when the difference of maximum and average field length is low and compressibility is high. VARCHAR(n) is more efficient when the difference of maximum and average field length is high and compressibility is low. We discuss multi-value compression further in another chapter.

Appendix D - Stored Procedure Example

Purpose

This Appendix lists the entire code for the CRE_STAGE stored procedure. This stored procedure is discussed in painful detail in the chapter on writing effective Stored Procedures. This Stored Procedure creates a STAGE table, or any table for that matter as another table without the Secondary Indices.

In order for this Stored Procedure to compile, you must log on as the owner of the procedure first. The following GRANTS are needed for this stored procedure to work. SELECT must be granted on DBC and the SOURCE database to the procedure owner WITH GRANT OPTION. Lastly, CREATE and DROP TABLE access must be granted on the STAGE database.

Grants Example

```
GRANT SELECT ON DBC TO CSQL_PROC WITH GRANT OPTION;
GRANT SELECT ON SOURCE_DB TO CSQL_PROC WITH GRANT OPTION;
GRANT TABLE ON CSQL_CLASS TO CSQL_PROC WITH GRANT OPTION;
```

Stored Procedure Code Example

```
REPLACE PROCEDURE CSQL_PROC.CRE_STAGE (
  IN    STG_DB       VARCHAR(60),       -- Stage DB
  IN    SRC_DB       VARCHAR(60),       -- Source DB
  IN    TAB_NM       VARCHAR(60),       -- Table Nm
  OUT   Orc          INTEGER,           -- Return Code
  OUT   Omsg         VARCHAR(10000)     -- Output Message
)
BEGIN
/* Program Designer:  Your Name                    Date: July 25, 2009

   Important facts:
-- Until V12, compile as owner of the procedure due to dynamic SQL.
-- Owner must have SEL granted on DBC and SOURCE DB with GRANT OPTION as such:
    -- GRANT SEL ON DBC TO CSQL_PROC WITH GRANT OPTION;
    -- GRANT SEL ON CSQL_CLASS TO CSQL_PROC WITH GRANT OPTION;
    --  Owner must have CREATE TABLE access to Source DB as such:
```

```
--    GRANT TABLE ON CSQL_CLASS TO CSQL_PROC;

Purpose: To create STAGE table as a Target table with the same PI and no SIs. */

-- Variable Declaration Section
DECLARE RetCd       INTEGER  Default 0;
DECLARE Stmt        VARCHAR(10000);
DECLARE CursCnt     INTEGER  Default 0;
DECLARE ColNm       VARCHAR(100)  Default Null;
DECLARE TabTyp      CHAR(1)   Default Null;
DECLARE UniqueTyp   VARCHAR(10)   Default Null;
DECLARE PriorStmt   VARCHAR(10000) Default 'Stmt not set';

-- Cursor Declaration Section
DECLARE   ColCurs   SCROLL CURSOR FOR
SELECT TRIM(ColumnName)||
     CASE WHEN ColumnPosition = MAX(ColumnPosition)
                   OVER (PARTITION BY DatabaseName,TableName)
            THEN ' ' ELSE ',' END AS ColNm,
     CASE WHEN UniqueFlag = 'Y' THEN ' UNIQUE '
              ELSE '' END AS UniqueFlag
FROM  DBC.Indices
WHERE DataBaseName = ''|| :SRC_DB || ''
AND  TableName = ''|| :TAB_NM || ''  AND IndexType='P'
ORDER BY ColumnPosition;

/* Procedure Section */
Lab1:  BEGIN
DECLARE EXIT HANDLER FOR SQLEXCEPTION
BEGIN
   SET RetCd=SQLCODE;
   SET Orc=RetCd;
   SET Omsg='SQL ERROR - '|| RetCd ||' Executed following: '|| PriorStmt;
End;

-- Input parameter Validation Section

/*If  Stage DB name is null, then end with error*/
IF (STG_DB = '') or (STG_DB is Null) or (TRIM(STG_DB) is Null) THEN
   SET Omsg='No Stage Database was entered as 1st Param!';
   SET Orc=31;
   LEAVE Lab1;
END IF;

/*If  SRC or Source DB name is null , then end */
IF (SRC_DB = '') or (SRC_DB is Null) or (TRIM(SRC_DB) is Null) THEN
   SET Omsg='No Source Database was entered as 2nd Param!';
   SET Orc=32;
   LEAVE Lab1;
```

```
END IF;

/*If  Source table name is null, then end */
IF (TAB_NM = '') or (TAB_NM is Null) or (TRIM(TAB_NM) is Null) THEN
   SET Omsg='No Source Table was entered as 3rd Param!';
   SET Orc=33;
   LEAVE Lab1;
END IF;

--Validate Table existence and get Tablekind
BEGIN
   -- Declare Exit handler
   SET PriorStmt='SELECT  TableKind  INTO ... to get Table Kind';
   SELECT  TableKind  INTO :TabTyp
   FROM  DBC.Tables
   WHERE  DatabaseName = ''|| trim(:SRC_DB) || ''
       AND TABLENAME =  ''|| trim(:TAB_NM) || '';
END;

IF TabTyp IS NULL THEN
   SET Omsg= upper(trim(SRC_DB)) ||'.'||upper(trim(TAB_NM))||
        ' Table not found in Database!';
   SET Orc=35;
   LEAVE Lab1;
ELSE
    IF UPPER(TabTyp) <> 'T' THEN
        SET Omsg= 'Table Kind is: '||TabTyp ||
                    ' - Source must be a table and is not!';
        SET Orc=36;
        LEAVE Lab1;
    END IF;
END IF;

BEGIN      -- Drop Table here
     DECLARE CONTINUE HANDLER FOR SQLSTATE '42000'
     BEGIN
        SET RetCd=SQLCODE;
        SET Omsg='SQL ERROR -  '|| RetCd ||
                    ' OK to drop if does not exist! '|| Stmt;
     END;
     SET Stmt='DROP TABLE  ' ||UPPER(TRIM(STG_DB))  ||'.'
                ||UPPER(TRIM(TAB_NM)) ||';' ;
     CALL DBC.SysExecSQL (:Stmt);
END;

-- Start building CREATE TABLE DDL
SET Stmt = 'CREATE TABLE '|| UPPER(TRIM(STG_DB))||'.'||UPPER(TRIM(TAB_NM))||' AS '||
UPPER(TRIM(SRC_DB))||'.'||UPPER(TRIM(TAB_NM))||'  WITH NO DATA AND STATISTICS ';
```

```
-- Finish building the CREATE with the correct PI
SET PriorStmt='Open ColCurs for first time.';
OPEN ColCurs;
FETCH ColCurs INTO ColNm,UniqueTyp ;
-- CursCnt prevents infinite loop
WHILE (SQLCODE=0) AND (CursCnt < 10000) DO
    IF CursCnt = 0  /*First Column */  THEN
        SET Stmt = Stmt || UniqueTyp ||' PRIMARY INDEX (';
    END IF;
    SET Stmt = Stmt ||trim(ColNm);
    SET CursCnt = CursCnt+1;
    FETCH ColCurs INTO ColNm,UniqueTyp ;
END WHILE;
CLOSE ColCurs;

SET Stmt = Stmt ||');';
SET PriorStmt= Stmt;
CALL DBC.SysExecSQL (:Stmt);

SET Omsg=Stmt;
SET Orc=0;

END Lab1;
END;
```

Appendix E - Compression Script

Purpose

This Appendix lists the entire code for the COMPRESSION_ANALZER stored procedure. This stored procedure is referenced in the Compression chapter. This Stored Procedure creates an effective way to determine the best compression column value candidates.

In order for this Stored Procedure to compile, you must log on as the owner of the procedure first. The following GRANTS are needed for this stored procedure to work. SELECT must be granted on DBC and the SOURCE database to the procedure owner WITH GRANT OPTION. Lastly, CREATE and DROP TABLE access must be granted on the STAGE database.

Grants Example

```
GRANT SELECT ON DBC TO CSQL_PROC WITH GRANT OPTION;
GRANT SELECT ON SOURCE_DB TO CSQL_PROC WITH GRANT OPTION;
GRANT TABLE ON CSQL_CLASS TO CSQL_PROC WITH GRANT OPTION;
```

Compression Analyzer Stored Procedure Code Example

```
-- To call:

CALL CSQL_PROC.COMPRESSION_ANALYZER('CSQL_CLASS','TEST_COMP',rc,msg);

-- Work table needed before compile.
CREATE MULTISET TABLE CSQL_CLASS.COMP_ANALYSIS
(DB_NM       VARCHAR(60) NOT NULL,
TAB_NM       VARCHAR(60) NOT NULL,
COL_NM       VARCHAR(60) NOT NULL,
COMP_VAL     VARCHAR(32767),
VAL_CNT      DECIMAL(25,3) NOT NULL,
FREQ         DECIMAL(25,3) NOT NULL,
CALC_DT      DATE  NOT NULL FORMAT 'YYYY-MM-DD')
PRIMARY INDEX COMP_ANALYSIS_P (DB_NM,TAB_NM);


REPLACE PROCEDURE  CSQL_PROC.COMPRESSION_ANALYZER
```

```
(
  IN     DB_IN        VARCHAR(60),        -- DatabaseName
  IN     TAB_IN       VARCHAR(60),        -- TableName
  OUT    Orc          INTEGER,            -- Return Code
  OUT    Omsg         VARCHAR(10000)      -- Output message
)
BEGIN
/* Program Designer:  Your Name                          Date: July 25, 2009

  Important facts:
   -- Until V12, compile as owner of the procedure due to dynamic SQL.
   -- Owner must have SELECT granted on DBC and Table DB with GRANT OPTION as such:
   --    GRANT SEL ON DBC TO CSQL_PROC WITH GRANT OPTION;
   --    GRANT SEL ON CSQL_CLASS TO CSQL_PROC WITH GRANT OPTION;
   -- You will get compile warnings due to volatile table creation and access,
      but this is OK;

Purpose: This procedure analyzes a table to determine possible compression candidates. */

-- Variable Declaration Section
DECLARE RetCd        INTEGER  Default 0;
DECLARE Stmt         VARCHAR(30000) DEFAULT ' ';
DECLARE DbId         VARBYTE(8);
DECLARE TabId        VARBYTE(8);
DECLARE UpperLimit   DECIMAL(9,3);
DECLARE FullTabNm    VARCHAR(125);
DECLARE Cntr         INTEGER  DEFAULT 0;
DECLARE FieldNm      VARCHAR(60);
DECLARE MaxL         DECIMAL(25,3);
DECLARE CursCnt      INTEGER  DEFAULT 0;
DECLARE TabTyp       CHAR(1)   Default Null;
DECLARE PriorStmt    VARCHAR(30000) Default 'Stmt not set';

/* Procedure Section */
Lab1:  BEGIN
DECLARE EXIT HANDLER FOR SQLEXCEPTION
Begin
   SET RetCd=SQLCODE;
   SET Orc=RetCd;
   SET Omsg='SQL ERROR - '|| RetCd ||' Executed following: '|| PriorStmt;
End;

-- Input parameter Validation Section

 /*If  DB_IN name is null, then end with error*/
IF (DB_IN = '') or (DB_IN is Null) or (TRIM(DB_IN) is Null) THEN
   SET Omsg='ERROR: No Database was entered as 1st Param!';
   SET Orc=31;
   LEAVE Lab1;
```

```
END IF;

 /*If  TAB_IN name is null, then end with error*/
IF (TAB_IN = '') or (TAB_IN is Null) or (TRIM(TAB_IN) is Null) THEN
   SET Omsg='ERROR: No Database was entered as 1st Param!';
   SET Orc=32;
   LEAVE Lab1;
END IF;

--Validate Table existence and get Tablekind
BEGIN
   -- You can declare an Exit handler here
   SET PriorStmt='SELECT  TableKind  INTO ... to get Table Kind and existence';
   SELECT tvm.DatabaseId,tvm.TVMId, tvm.Tablekind
   INTO :DbId,:TabId,:TabTyp
   FROM DBC.tvm JOIN DBC.dbase
   ON  tvm.DatabaseId = dbase.DatabaseId
       AND dbase.DatabaseName=:DB_IN
       AND tvm.TVMName=:TAB_IN;
END;

IF TabTyp IS NULL THEN
   SET Omsg= 'ERROR: '||UPPER(TRIM(DB_IN)) ||'.'||UPPER(TRIM(TAB_IN))|| ' Table not found
in Database!';
   SET Orc=35;
   LEAVE Lab1;
ELSE
    IF UPPER(TabTyp) <> 'T' THEN
        SET Omsg= 'ERROR: Table Kind is: '||TabTyp || ' - Input must be a table and is not!';
        SET Orc=36;
        LEAVE Lab1;
    END IF;
END IF;

SET FullTabNm = TRIM(DB_IN)||'.'||TRIM(TAB_IN);

-- Get the row count of the table and exit if less than 500 rows
-- Create a volatile table to capture the table row count
SET PriorStmt='CREATE VOLATILE TABLE VOL_ROWS...';
CREATE VOLATILE TABLE VOL_ROWS
          (Cnt INT)  ON COMMIT PRESERVE ROWS;

SET Stmt = 'INS INTO VOL_ROWS
              SEL ZEROIFNULL(COUNT(*))
              FROM '||TRIM(DB_IN)||'.'||TRIM(TAB_IN)||';';
SET PriorStmt='INS INTO VOL_ROWS...';
CALL DBC.SysExecSQL(:Stmt);

SET PriorStmt='SEL Cnt  INTO :Cntr FROM VOL_ROWS;';
```

```
SEL Cnt  INTO :Cntr FROM VOL_ROWS;
IF Cntr < 500 THEN
   SET Omsg='ERROR: Table is less than 500 rows!';
   LEAVE Lab1;
END IF;

-- Clean out the COMP_ANALYSIS table for this entry
SET PriorStmt='DELETE FROM CSQL_CLASS.COMP_ANALYSIS...';
DEL FROM CSQL_CLASS.COMP_ANALYSIS
WHERE DB_NM = :DB_IN AND TAB_NM = :TAB_IN;

--  Insert any current compression values
SET PriorStmt='INSERT INTO CSQL_CLASS.COMP_ANALYSIS...';
INS INTO CSQL_CLASS.COMP_ANALYSIS
  SEL TRIM(:DB_IN) ,TRIM(:TAB_IN),TRIM(FieldName),
   '*** COMPRESSION ALREADY EXISTS: '||TRIM(CompressValueList),
   0 ,0,CURRENT_DATE
  FROM DBC.TVFields
  WHERE DatabaseId = :DbId
   AND TableId = :TabId
   AND CompressValueList IS NOT NULL;

BEGIN
  -- Cursor Declaration Section
DECLARE   ColCurs   SCROLL CURSOR FOR
SEL FieldName,MaxLength
FROM DBC.TVFields
WHERE DatabaseId=:DbId
     AND TableId=:TabId
     AND FieldId NOT IN
     -- Not PI or PPI
     (SEL FieldId FROM DBC.INDEXES
      WHERE DatabaseId=:DbId
            AND TableId=:TabId
            AND IndexType IN ('P','Q'))
      -- Not Variable Length
      AND FieldType NOT IN ('BO','BV','CO','CV')
ORDER BY FieldId;

--  Analyze each column in the table
SET PriorStmt='Open ColCurs for first time.';
OPEN ColCurs;
FETCH ColCurs INTO FieldNm,MaxL;
-- CursCnt prevents infinite loop
WHILE (SQLCODE=0) AND (CursCnt < 10000) DO
      SET UpperLimit = .125 / CAST(MaxL AS DECIMAL(25,3));
      SET Stmt = ' INS INTO CSQL_CLASS.COMP_ANALYSIS
             SEL '''||TRIM(DB_IN)||''','''||TRIM(TAB_IN)||''',
               '''||TRIM(FieldNm)||''',
```

```
            CAST(ColValue AS VARCHAR(32767)),
            VAL_CNT,Frequency,CURRENT_DATE
          FROM (SEL '||TRIM(FieldNm)||' AS ColValue
            ,CAST(COUNT(*) AS DECIMAL(25,3)) as VAL_CNT
            ,VAL_CNT/'||CAST(Cntr AS VARCHAR(25))||' AS Frequency
             FROM '||FullTabNm||'
             GROUP BY 1
             HAVING Frequency>'||CAST(UpperLimit AS VARCHAR(25))||') a
          QUALIFY row_number() over (ORDER BY VAL_CNT DESC ) <= 255;';
    CALL DBC.SysExecSQL(:Stmt);
    SET CursCnt = CursCnt+1;
    FETCH ColCurs INTO FieldNm,MaxL;
END WHILE;
CLOSE ColCurs;

END;

-- Drop Volatile table
BEGIN
     DECLARE CONTINUE HANDLER FOR SQLSTATE '42000'
     BEGIN
        SET RetCd=SQLCODE;
        SET Omsg='SQL ERROR -  '|| RetCd ||' OK to drop if does not exist! '|| Stmt;
     END;

     DROP TABLE VOL_ROWS;
END;

 SET Omsg='Compression Analysis finished! Query as follows:
SELECT * FROM CSQL_CLASS.COMP_ANALYSIS
WHERE DB_NM='''||TRIM(DB_IN)||''' AND TAB_NM='''||TRIM(TAB_IN)||
''' ORDER BY 1,2,3,5 DESC;';

END Lab1;
END;
```

Appendix F - UNIX, LINUX, Windows Command Conversion Charts

Purpose

This appendix provides a cross-reference guide for useful MP-RAS and Linux commands. The primary areas of focus will be as follows:

- Common user commands
- System administration related commands
- Disk and File system related commands
- Network and Connectivity commands
- Performance and Tuning for the OS
- Hardware information and status commands
- Debugging and dump analysis tools
- Teradata and PDE specific tools

Section	MP-RAS - 32 Bit	Linux - 64 Bit	Explanation
Getting Help			
	man	man, info	The man command works similar on both operating systems. In addition, Linux has the info command. When invoked, man, brings up a text-based hyperlink type interface.
	<command> -?	<command> --help	This command will invoke help. MP-RAS uses -?, and Linux uses --help.
	find	find locate updatedb	The find command works similar in both MP-RAS and Linux. Linux also has the locate command. These commands can be faster because it stores the information on a database. However, this database needs to be updated.

Section	MP-RAS - 32 Bit	Linux - 64 Bit	Explanation
Networking Commands			
	rlogin, rsh, rexec, telnet	ssh	Both operating systems have secure protocols which should be used.
	rcp ftp	scp sftp, ftp	Both operating systems have secure protocols which should be used. FTP can still be used for anonymous use.
	rlogin telnet	rlogin telnet	The rlogin and telnet commands are still available. However, this functionality is disabled by default on the Linux node.
Performance / Statistics / Tuning Commands			
	/etc/gsc/bin/top	top	Top works similar on both operating systems.
	sar	sar mpstat vmstat	Sar works similar on both operating systems. When invoked, sar will obtain valuable information on processor, memory, and disk statistics.
	memsize	free vmstat /proc/meminfo	Memsize in MP-RAS along with the free, vmstat, and /proc/meminfo on Linux will output the amount of memory available to the system.
	pinfo -v	/proc/cpuinfo mpstat	Pinfo in MP-RAS along with cpuinfo and mpstat command will provide sar-like processor usage information.
	/etc/conf/cf.d/mtune /etc/conf/cf.d/stune	sysctl /etc/sysctl.conf /proc/sys	Kernel tuning is very different between both operating systems. MP-RAS typically requires a kernel rebuild with every tuning change. However, Linux can change tuning parameters seamlessly by using the sysctl. In Linux, you can easily browse the kernel parameters in the /proc/sys/ file system unlike mtune and stune that is done via cat commands.

Section	MP-RAS - 32 Bit	Linux - 64 Bit	Explanation
Disk and Filesystem commands			
	mount mount -F cdfs ...	mount mount [-t <type>] ...	Mount works similar in both operating systems. In Linux, you do need to specify the files system type with the mount command.
	dfspace, df, du	df, du	The dfspace is for MP-RAS only but the df, and du commands are the equivalent for both operating systems. These commands will report the disk space used for each mounted file system.
	prtvtoc -f <file> <dev>	sfdisk -d <dev> > <file>	This command will print the partition table to a file, which can be modified and copied back. This is similar to the sfdisk command in Linux.
	edvtoc -f <file> <dev>	sfdisk -d <dev> < <file>	Both commands will enable us to take the prtvtoc file changes and write the file back to the partition table on disk.
	prtvtoc <dev>	fdisk -l <dev>	These commands provide a simple way to print the partition table to the screen.
	fsck	fsck	File system check
	mkfs	mkfs	Command to make a file system
	swap -l	swapon -s	Displays the swap configuration and size. This command can also create more swap.
	/etc/vfstab	/etc/fstab	Configuration table that show files system layout
	dkconfig	/opt/teradata/lsituil/lsi util raidmon (daemon)	lsiutil and dkconfig can be used to check the disk status and along with modify the raid configuration.

Section	MP-RAS - 32 Bit	Linux - 64 Bit	Explanation
User and System Administration			
	<del>	<cntl-c>	The default "interrupt" character. The Linux equivalent is Control-C
	stty	stty	TTY Setup is pretty much the same in both OS's.
	/etc/.osm /etc/.osm.old usererr & streams	/var/log/boot.msg, dmesg /var/log/boot.omsg /var/log/messages	Linux logs all messages to /var/log/messages which displays similar information to streams and usererr in MP-RAS. The equivalent to /etc/.osm is show with the dmesg.
	while true; do > <something> > sleep 2 > done	watch <something>	These commands displays - by default - output every 2 seconds.
	script	script replay	These commands are similar in both operating system which allows users to replay a script and watch it in real time.
	pg, more	less, more	Equivalent commands which enables you to limit results to a page.
OS Shell			
	cpio	cpio, tar	archive
	compress	gzip, bzip2	compress
	cat /etc/.relid	SPident, cat /etc/SuSE-release	OS version
	tweak, didle, anlz		Change kernel memory
	kill	kill	kill a process
	who -b	who -b	last time system was rebooted

Section	MP-RAS - 32 Bit	Linux - 64 Bit	Explanation
OS Shell			
	/etc/rcX.d/<script>	chkconfig, /etc/init.d	startup scripts
	ps	ps	process info
	shutdown	poweroff, reboot, shutdown	shutdown a node
	fdump -l	grep DUMPDEV /etc/sysconfig/dump	dump location
	dumpsave	lkcd save	save OS dump
	devstat -F	lsscsi	Lists SCSI devices that are attached
	pcixplore, pcidev, pcislot	lspci, scanpci	Lists PCI devices that are installed
		lsusb	Lists USB devices that are attached
	sel	showsel	Displays the Server Event Log
Debugging / OS Dump			
	crash	lcrash	Crash dump analysis tool
	gdb	/usr/pde/bin/gdb	Debugger
	truss	strace	Trace system calls of a program
		ltrace	Trace library calls of a program
	fuser	fuser, lsof	The fuser command works similar in both operating systems by displaying the processes that have a file open.
Teradata Commands			
	pdestate	pdestate	Display the state of PDE/TDBMS.
	pcl, psh	pcl, psh	PCL and PSH work similar in both operating systems that secure protocols in the background.
	xctl -nw	ctl	CTL is similar in both operating systems. Help you control your interaction with the system
	vprocmanager	vprocmanager	List Teradata configuration information

Section	MP-RAS - 32 Bit	Linux - 64 Bit	Explanation
Teradata Commands			
	cnsterm cnstool	cnsterm cnstool	Command line terminal option
	/tpasw	/opt/teradata/tdat/tdbms	TDBMS software install location
	/tpasw/bin	/usr/tdbms/bin	TDBMS bin
	/nssoft/unix-soft/<version>	/opt/teradata/tdat/pde	PDE software install location
	/usr/ntos/bin	/usr/pde/bin	PDE bin
	/nssoft/tgtw/<version>	/opt/teradata/tdat/tgtw	gateway
	activate_pde		Activate PDE version
	activate_abe	vmf_activate <BE NAME>	Activate alternate boot env
	tdpkgrm	tdpkgrm	Remove TD pkg
	/etc/inet/hosts	/etc/hosts	hosts file
	machinetype	n/a	
	uname	uname	System name
	/etc/smainfo	/etc/opt/teradata/sm3g/smainfo	Location of PMAID-MPP Configurations
	/etc/pmaid	/etc/opt/teradata/bynet/pmaid	Location of PMAID-SMP Configurations
	blmd -p	blmd -p	Current active PMA ID
	psh	psh	parallel shell
	pcl	pcl	parallel command language
	bam	bam	bynet administrative menu
	bam -s	bam -s	bynet status
	vconfig -x vp		display vprocconfig.gdo
	vconfig -x vc		Display vconfig.gdo
	xctl	ctl	Display controlgdo
	puma	puma	

Section	MP-RAS - 32 Bit	Linux - 64 Bit	Explanation
Teradata Commands			
	/usr/ntos/bin/tpatrace	tpatrace	TPA trace
	verify_pdisks	verify_pdisks	verify pdisks
	/dev/pdisk	/dev/pdisk	location of pdisks
	/ntos/vconfig.out	/etc/opt/teradata/tdconfig/vconfig.out	location of vconfig.out
GDO's			
	/ntos/*.gdo	/etc/opt/teradata/tdconfig/	GDO location
		pdepath -c	GDO location
	control.gdo	control.gdo	control.gdo
	system.gdo	system.gdo	system.gdo
	vconfig.gdo	vconfig.gdo	vconfig.gdo
	vprocconfig.gdo	vprocconfig.gdo	vprocconfig.gdo
	/var/ns/bkup/*.gdo	/etc/opt/teradata/tdconfig/Backup	GDO backup location
TPA Commands			
	/etc/init.d/tpa start	/etc/init.d/tpa start	Start PDE/DBS
	/etc/init.d/tpa stop	/etc/init.d/tpa stop	Stop PDE/DBS
	tpareset -f <reason>	tpareset -f <reason>	TPA reset
	tpareset -x <reason>	tpareset -x <reason>	Shutdown PDE/DBS
	/usr/ntos/bin/tpareset -d	/usr/pde/bin/tpareset -d	restart with dump
	recond -nofiles -nogdo		Run reconcile without start
	/tpasw/etc/tpastartup	/opt/teradata/tdat/tdbms/<ver>/etc/startup.txt	tpastartup file
	/etc/rc3.d/S50tpa	/etc/init.d/tpa	TPA init script

Section	MP-RAS - 32 Bit	Linux - 64 Bit	Explanation
TPA Commands			
	mv /etc/rc3.d/S50tpa to something else	chkconfig tpa off	Manual Start
	/usr/ntos/bin/pdestate	/usr/pde/bin/pdestate	show pde state
		/usr/pde/bin/pdestate -a	show pde and dbs state
	/usr/ntos/bin/tpasetcfg	/usr/pde/bin/tpasetcfg	Start with available nodes
PDEstate Commands			
	Null	Down	
	Notpa	Start	
	Notpa/Netconfig	Start/Netconfig	
	Notpa/Netready	Start/Netready, Start/Gdosync and Start/ Sysgdoinit.	
	Notpa/Reconcile	Start/Reconcile	
	Tpa/Start	Start/Vprocalloc, Start/Fsgdevinit, Start/Vprocstart, Start/Fsgdevopen	
	Tpa/Vprocs	Start/vprocdone, Start/Startcns and Run/Starttpa	
	Tpa/Ready	Run/Ready	
	Tpa	Run/Started	
		Reset_Begin	Reset in progress
		Reset_Stoptasks	
		Reset_Pdedump	
		Reset_Killtasks	
		Reset_Network	
		Reset_Vprocstop	
		Reset_Fsgflush	
		Reset_Final	

Section	MP-RAS - 32 Bit	Linux - 64 Bit	Explanation
PDEstate Commands			
		Down_Notstarted	System never started
		Down_Savetrace	Saves tpatrace buffers
		Down_Softstop	
		Down_Shutdown	Down after tpareset –x
		Down_Hardstop	PDE is down
	/dev/pdisk	/dev/pdisk	location of pdisks
	/ntos/vconfig.out	/etc/opt/teradata/tdconfig/vconfig.out	location of vconfig.out
Crashdumps			
	/dev/pdedump	/var/opt/teradata/tddump/	PDE dump slice
		/usr/pde/bin/pdepath -D	PDE crashdump location
	dbgcsp -E		show dumps in database
	pdedumpcheck		
	csp -mode list -source table		
	pdedumpspace		
		/usr/pde/bin/csp -mode list	look for crashdumps
		/usr/pde/bin/csp -force -mode save	save dumps
		/usr/pde/bin/csp -mode clear -source <dump>	delete a crashdump

Section	MP-RAS - 32 Bit	Linux - 64 Bit	Explanation
Crashdumps			
		/usr/pde/bin/csp -mode clear -source <table>	To delete a dump from the dbc.crashdumps user specify the source to be table
		/usr/pde/bin/tpareset -p <reason>	Force a node to panic and take crashdump
		/usr/pde/bin/tpareset -n -p <reason>	Force a node to panic, but don't take crashdump
Hardware			
	/var/array/logs	none	Disk Array Logs. MP-RAS ONLY
	ripm, ripb, ripc	none	DA Controller status. MP-RAS ONLY
	acf, ace	none	Disk Array Configuration. MP-RAS ONLY
	apc, apr, apcheckall	none	Array Parity Check. MP-RAS ONLY
	/usr/sbin/SYS_dump <SMPXXX-Y>	none	Initiate dump remotely. MP-RAS ONLY
	/usr/sbin/SYS_reset <SMPXXX-Y>	none	Initiate reset remotely. MP-RAS ONLY
GSCTOOLS			
	GSCTOOLS	teradata-gsctools	GSC tools package
	getCylDocs.pl	getCylDocs.pl	
	dumplook	dumplook.sh	
	perflook	perflook.sh	
	cc_check	sys_val.pl	
	tam	n/a	

INDEX

H

I

J

L

M

N

O

P

Q

R

S

T

U

V

W